Company to Company

A task-based approach to business
emails, letters and faxes

Fourth Edition

Student's Book

Andrew Littlejohn

CAMBRIDGE
UNIVERSITY PRESS

University Printing House, Cambridge CB2 8BS, United Kingdom

One Liberty Plaza, 20th Floor, New York, NY 10006, USA

477 Williamstown Road, Port Melbourne, VIC 3207, Australia

314–321, 3rd Floor, Plot 3, Splendor Forum, Jasola District Centre, New Delhi – 110025, India

79 Anson Road, #06–04/06, Singapore 079906

Cambridge University Press is part of the University of Cambridge.

It furthers the University's mission by disseminating knowledge in the pursuit of education, learning and research at the highest international levels of excellence.

www.cambridge.org
Information on this title: www.cambridge.org/9780521609753

First published 2005
Reprinted 2018

Printed in Italy by Rotolito S.p.A.

A catalogue record for this publication is available from the British Library

ISBN 978-0-521-60975-3 Student's Book
ISBN 978-0-521-60976-0 Teacher's Book

To Lita, without whom I doubt this book or my writing career would ever have happened; Daniel, aged 1½, who almost made the writing of the first edition of this book impossible; Fiona, whose imminent arrival kept me working; and David, who arrived just in time for the second edition. Since then, there's been the third edition and now the fourth edition, and Daniel is now 20, Fiona is now 18 and David is now 12. As they've grown, so has **Company to Company***.*

Acknowledgements

Thanks to Diana Hicks, whose energy and imagination first gave me the idea, and all the Al Jalahmas, particularly Anne and Yousuf, and the staff at Arabian Electronics who helped me with original source material. I am also indebted to many people at CUP who over the years have given useful guidance and support. For the fourth edition, I would particularly like to thank Clare Abbott, Elin Jones and Catriona Watson-Brown, who steered the typescript into production.

The author and publishers would also like to thank the following people and teaching centres who have given very useful feedback on *Company to Company*: Bell School, Cambridge; Bell College, Saffron Walden; British Council, Munich; Cambridge Eurocentre; Colchester English Study Centre; Jim Corbett, Key English Language Services, Sweden; Godmer House, Oxford; S. Hagen, Newcastle Polytechnic; Inlingua School of Languages, Hove; Münchner Volkshochschule, Munich; Grant Trew, Osaka, Japan; Ton Wageman, The Netherlands; Sue Spencer, Indonesia; Pam Scott, Thailand; Anne Weber, Switzerland; Vincent Broderick, Osaka, Japan. Thanks also to Peter Donovan, Will Capel, Sarah Almy, Jayshree Ramsurun, Ellen Shaw at CUP and James Dale and Amanda Maris for freelance editorial work.

Note on the Fourth Edition

For the fourth edition of *Company to Company*, both the Student's Book and the Teacher's Book have been completely reset with improvements in the design. Many additions have also been made to the text. The course includes new guidance on writing emails, British and American English usage, style, levels of formality and politeness, customer-service language, inviting and responding to invitations, use of paragraphs and other language points. Two new sections have been added to further develop the students' ability to edit their own work. All of the innovations introduced in previous editions are still there, of course, including the self-test tasks at the start of each unit, the guided work in the *Study sections*, the fluency-focused *Activity sections* and *The writing process* sections.

We welcome your comments on using *Company to Company*. Please write to Andrew Littlejohn, c/o ELT, Cambridge University Press, The Edinburgh Building, Shaftesbury Road, Cambridge CB2 2RU, England. Fax: +44 1223 325984, email eltmail@cambridge.org.

You are also welcome to visit the website which Andrew Littlejohn maintains, where articles, papers and an A–Z of ELT methodology are available: www.AndrewLittlejohn.net

Contents

To the student

Please read this first! (Teachers, too!)

Company to Company is probably very different from other books that you have used to learn English, so it may help if you read this introduction first.

The book has eight units. Each unit is divided into three different sections.

Section A is the *Study section*. At the beginning of the section, you can do a self-test in the form of a letter- or email-writing exercise. You can then learn phrases for writing business correspondence. At the end of the section, there is another writing exercise. These beginning and end exercises will show you how much you have learned in the section.

Section B is the *Activity section*. This helps you to practise writing in a 'real' situation. Here, you can use everything you learned in Section A. In the activity, the class is divided into groups. Each group is one of three 'companies' in a business situation (for example, buying or selling something). In your group, you have to write messages to the other 'companies' using the role cards at the back of the book (see page 86). There are three cards for each group in each activity, and your teacher will tell you which card to look at next. The role cards and the messages that you get from other groups give you new information and, together, you will have to make decisions before you write. Your company is trying to get its business done, so you will have to think and write as quickly as possible!

To get maximum benefit from the activity, it is important that **everyone in your group writes**. Once the activity is over, you can look back at your own messages and the messages written by other students to see if you can improve them.

Section C is *The writing process* section. This shows you how you can develop your abilities in writing, how you can plan and revise letters and help yourself to write better English.

At the back of the book, there is an *Index of model letters, emails and key words* that you can use in class, at work or at home. This will help you to find an example letter or email or a particular word. There is also a *Summary of useful phrases and main points* from each unit and a *Letter and email layout guide*.

We hope you learn a lot from this book and enjoy using it.

Unit 1 Making enquiries

1A Study section

- emails
- opening and closing a message
- subject headings
- asking for and sending information
- email style
- being polite

Test yourself

You want a new printer for your computer. You have seen an advertisement for the Solar EX43. Write an email to Computer World, sales@computerworld.com, and ask them how much the printer costs and how long they would take to deliver it. Write a complete email, with a subject heading, names, etc. (Invent any details you need.)

When you have finished, put the message away until the end of this section.

1.1 Intercity Bank ask for catalogues

Read this message and the one on page 8.

a   Why does Jennifer Long want the catalogues?
b   Mr Basuki is sending something in the post and something with his email. What?
c   Why do you think Jakarta Furnishings offer a 5% discount for web sales?

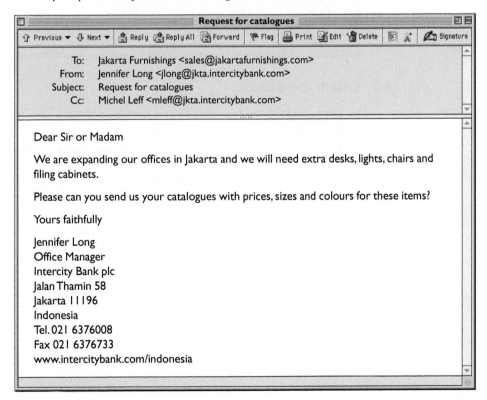

Request for catalogues

Previous ▼ | Next ▼ | Reply | Reply All | Forward | Flag | Print | Edit | Delete | | A' | Signature

To: Jakarta Furnishings <sales@jakartafurnishings.com>
From: Jennifer Long <jlong@jkta.intercitybank.com>
Subject: Request for catalogues
Cc: Michel Leff <mleff@jkta.intercitybank.com>

Dear Sir or Madam

We are expanding our offices in Jakarta and we will need extra desks, lights, chairs and filing cabinets.

Please can you send us your catalogues with prices, sizes and colours for these items?

Yours faithfully

Jennifer Long
Office Manager
Intercity Bank plc
Jalan Thamin 58
Jakarta 11196
Indonesia
Tel. 021 6376008
Fax 021 6376733
www.intercitybank.com/indonesia

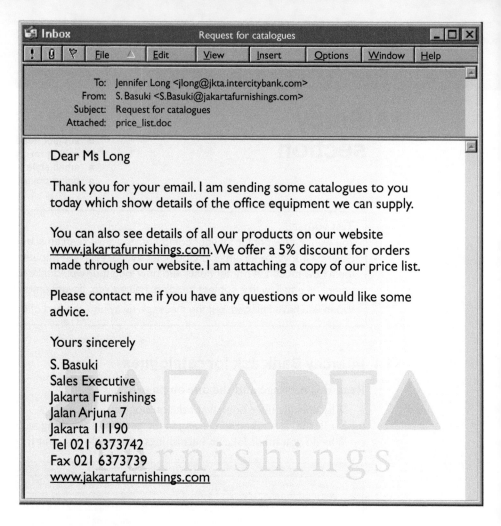

Inbox — Request for catalogues

! | File | Edit | View | Insert | Options | Window | Help

To: Jennifer Long <jlong@jkta.intercitybank.com>
From: S. Basuki <S.Basuki@jakartafurnishings.com>
Subject: Request for catalogues
Attached: price_list.doc

Dear Ms Long

Thank you for your email. I am sending some catalogues to you today which show details of the office equipment we can supply.

You can also see details of all our products on our website www.jakartafurnishings.com. We offer a 5% discount for orders made through our website. I am attaching a copy of our price list.

Please contact me if you have any questions or would like some advice.

Yours sincerely

S. Basuki
Sales Executive
Jakarta Furnishings
Jalan Arjuna 7
Jakarta 11190
Tel 021 6373742
Fax 021 6373739
www.jakartafurnishings.com

1.2 Email: the basics

1 Look back at the two emails and match each item (1–7) to the correct meaning (a–g).

1	To:	a	A document or other file you want to send with the email
2	From:	b	The name and email address of the person you are writing to
3	Subject:	c	The name and email address of someone you want to send a 'blind copy' to (i.e. the other people who receive the message can't see that this person has also received a copy)
4	Cc:		
5	Bcc:	d	Your full name, address and other details that are automatically put at the end of your email
		e	The topic you are writing about
6	Attached:	f	Your name and email address
7	Signature	g	The name and email address of someone you want to send a copy to

2 Notice the layout of the email messages.

a Where does each paragraph start?
b How are the paragraphs separated?
c How does the email open and close?

1.3 *Dear ... / Yours ...*

Here are some ways to start your message.

Dear Sir or Madam	*to a company*
Dear Sir	*to a man if you do not know his name*
Dear Madam	*to a woman if you do not know her name*
Dear Mr Smith	*to a married or unmarried man*
Dear Ms Smith	*to a married or unmarried woman*
Dear Mrs Smith	*to a married woman*
Dear Miss Smith	*to an unmarried woman*
Dear John	*to a friend or someone you know well*

Writing tip Be careful how you open a message.

- Do not use *Mr/Mrs/Ms* with a first name (e.g. *Dear Mr John* is not correct).
- Unless you know that a woman prefers to be called *Miss* or *Mrs*, use *Ms*.

The way you close a message depends on how you open it.

Dear Sir or Madam	Yours faithfully
Dear Mr/Ms/Mrs/Miss Smith	Yours sincerely
Dear John	Best wishes

Choose the correct close from the box for each of the openings (a–g).

Best wishes	Yours faithfully	Yours sincerely

a Dear Mrs Wilson   e Dear Mr González
b Dear Madam   f Dear David
c Dear Ms Hemsuchi   g Dear Sir or Madam
d Dear Susanna

1.4 Subject headings

Writing tip Many businesses receive hundreds of emails every day. Unfortunately, a lot of these messages are 'junk mail', usually advertising. Many people do not even open these messages – they delete them straight away. For this reason, it is important that your emails have a short, clear subject heading which encourages the reader to open the message. This can also help to ensure that the message goes to the right person.

What subject headings can you put for these messages (a–d)?

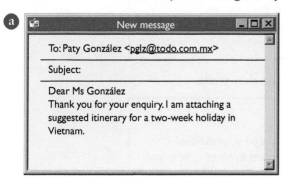

a

To: Paty González <pglz@todo.com.mx>

Subject:

Dear Ms González
Thank you for your enquiry. I am attaching a suggested itinerary for a two-week holiday in Vietnam.

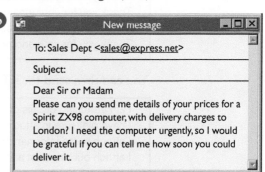

b

To: Sales Dept <sales@express.net>

Subject:

Dear Sir or Madam
Please can you send me details of your prices for a Spirit ZX98 computer, with delivery charges to London? I need the computer urgently, so I would be grateful if you can tell me how soon you could deliver it.

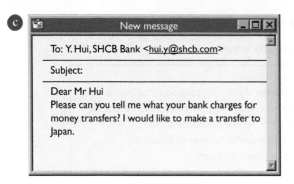

c

To: Y. Hui, SHCB Bank <hui.y@shcb.com>

Subject:

Dear Mr Hui
Please can you tell me what your bank charges for money transfers? I would like to make a transfer to Japan.

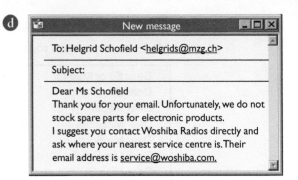

d

To: Helgrid Schofield <helgrids@mzg.ch>

Subject:

Dear Ms Schofield
Thank you for your email. Unfortunately, we do not stock spare parts for electronic products.
I suggest you contact Woshiba Radios directly and ask where your nearest service centre is. Their email address is service@woshiba.com.

1.5 Practice

What's wrong with this email? Look at 1.1–1.4 again and write it out correctly.

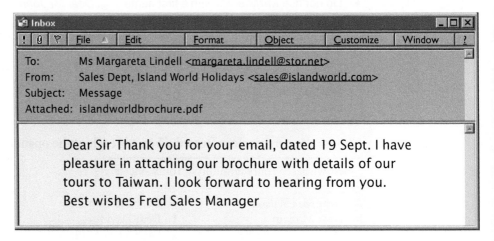

To: Ms Margareta Lindell <margareta.lindell@stor.net>
From: Sales Dept, Island World Holidays <sales@islandworld.com>
Subject: Message
Attached: islandworldbrochure.pdf

Dear Sir Thank you for your email, dated 19 Sept. I have pleasure in attaching our brochure with details of our tours to Taiwan. I look forward to hearing from you. Best wishes Fred Sales Manager

1.6 Asking for and sending information

You can ask for information in different ways.

Please can you tell me …
Please can you send me …
Please can you send me details of …

If you are replying, you can first thank the person for their message.

Thank you for your email.
Thank you for your email, dated 6 June.
Many thanks for your message, dated 6 June.
Thank you for your enquiry.

You can then send the information they want.

I am attaching details of …
I have pleasure in attaching …
I attach some information which I hope you find useful.
I attach our price list and look forward to hearing from you.

You work for a company that sells mobile phones. What can you write in these situations?

a Someone has written asking for details of mobile phones that include a camera.
b Someone has written to ask you for details of the types of accounts you offer.
c You want to know more information about the new MI300 Henrison mobile phone and when it will be available.
d The air conditioner in your shop doesn't work. You want a list of service centres.

1.7 Message style

Writing tip There are many different styles of writing. For a student of English, this can be a problem, because if you use the wrong style, you can cause offence or give the wrong impression. For this reason, in *Company to Company* you will learn a style that you can use in most situations.

- Write in a natural style. Do not use an old-fashioned, very formal style. Say *Thank you for your letter, dated 14 June,* not *We have received your letter of the 14th of this month.*

- Do not use very informal language, unless you know the person well. Do not write *Hi!* or *Hello!* or *Ciao, John!* Write *Dear John* (if you know the person) or *Dear Mr Smith.*

- Do not use text-message abbreviations such as *I hope I can c u soon* or *Yr order is waiting 4 u.*

- Do not use slang. Write *Someone in the office can help,* not *A guy here can help.*

- Do not use 'emoticons'. Emoticons are symbols which people often use in Internet chat, such as :-) (happy), :-((sad).

What's wrong with these messages? Write them correctly.

a Hello, Steven!
   Thx for yr email. I'm gld u recvd the pkt OK. Great 2 hear u like the pics. :-)
b Dear Mr Wilson,
   We are in receipt of your message, dated 15th of this month. I can confirm that we have despatched your order according to your instructions.
c Hi there
   How r you? I've passed your msg to Bill, a guy in my office, and he'll contact you u soon. Bye.
d Dear Ms Brown
   We are awaiting your instructions concerning the address for the despatch of your order.

1.8 Practice

There are two things missing and two style problems in each of these messages. Check 1.1–1.7 again and complete and correct each message.

To:	Next Travel <info@nexttravel.com>
From:	Renate Makosch <r.makosch@observer.org>
Subject:	a ....
Attached:	pricelist.pdf

Dear Sir or Madam

This year, the Daily Observer newspaper will print a special report on travel agencies. We were wondering if you'd like to put an ad in it.

I attach our price list and look forward to hearing from you. :-)

b ....
Renate Makosch
Advertising Manager

To:	Ms I. Morales <IsabelMorales@iol.it>
From:	Tom Lander <tlander@sportscars.co.uk>
Subject:	c ....
Attached:	Swiftzx.doc

Hi!

Thank you for your email about the Swift ZX series sports cars.
I attach some information which I hope you will find useful.

Bye for now.

d ....

1.9 Be polite!

In business, if you are polite, you will usually get a better response and better service. Users of English often do the following to show politeness.

- Say please and thank you:
  Thank you for your email. Please can you send me your catalogue?
- Say more:
  Thank you for your order for 10 boxes of Sunlight Wallpaper. Our price for each box is $250, plus an additional $50 for postage. Our normal delivery time is 3–5 days, not *We got your order. The cost is $250 per box plus $50 for delivery. Delivery is 3–5 days.*
- Avoid being very direct:
  We think your prices are rather high, not *Your prices are not acceptable.*
- Ask rather than order:
  Please could you send it as soon as possible? not *You must send it straight away.*
- Use indirect questions:
  I was wondering if you could help me, not *Can you help me?*
- Avoid blaming or accusing the addressee:
  I am afraid there is a problem with the order, not *You've made a mistake with my order.*
- Understate the point:
  It seems we have a small problem, not *There is a problem.*

There are many examples of polite letters and emails in *Company to Company*. As you read them, compare with what you would say in your language.

These messages sound impolite in English. Make them more polite.

a Dear Mr Brown
   Your company delivered the goods very late. This is very bad service.
   Please deliver on time in future.
b Dear Sharon
   Let's meet next Monday at 1 p.m. We can meet at The Mousetrap restaurant.
   I have to leave at 2 p.m., so come on time.
c Dear Ms Mustapha
   I received your letter. I have sent the goods. You will get them on Tuesday.
d Mr Smith
   Send me your price list. I need it now, so send it immediately.
e What's your price for a Delphi ZX45 modem?

1.10 Consolidation: a complete email

You are the Purchasing Supervisor at Green Supermarkets. Your manager has just sent you this email. Write a polite email to Corona (sales@corona.com.nz) with a copy to your manager.

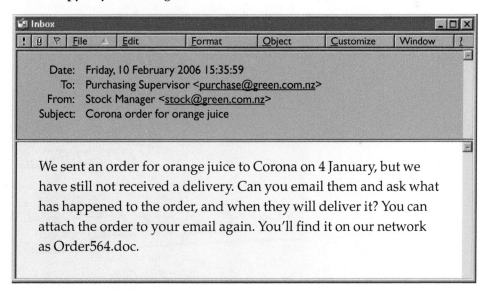

What have you learned?
Look back at the message you wrote to Computer World at the beginning of this section. Compare it with your message to Corona. Can you see an improvement?
Think about:
● email layout
● opening/close
● subject headings
● how to ask for information
● style
● politeness.

1B Activity section   Misplaced orders

1 Slembrouck BVBA, a wholesaler in Belgium, have problems. Business is not good, and they have dismissed a lot of staff. Their offices are now very disorganised. Here are some orders that their sales executive brought back after a trip to England. The orders are not clear. Answer the following questions.

a What have ABC (Drinks Machines) Ltd ordered?
b Who ordered the shampoo?
c How can you improve the layout of the orders so that it is clearer?

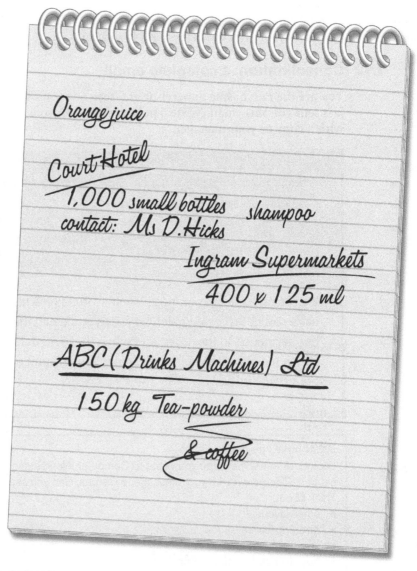

wholesaler
a business that buys goods in large quantities from the manufacturer and then sells them in smaller quantities to shops, etc.

2 The accounts department made out these invoices for the orders. Look at them and answer these questions.

a Are the invoices correct?

b If the Court Hotel want to write to Slembrouck BVBA, who will they address their email to? How will they open and close the email?

c If ABC (Drinks Machines) Ltd want to send a similar message, what will they write?

SLEMBROUCK
BVBA
Hoekstraat 250 9932 Ronsele Belgium
Tel 32-9-264-3794 Fax 32-9-264-4179
Order online at www.slembrouck.be
enquiries at info@slembrouck.be

Invoice No. 391	Date: 25 Jan	
Order No. 256	Contact: Stefaan Ghislain	

To: Court Hotel
     Chilcompton
     Bath BA3 4SA England

1,000 small bottles of shampoo			
@ €60 per 100	€	600	00
fixed delivery charge	€	40	00
TOTAL	€	640	00

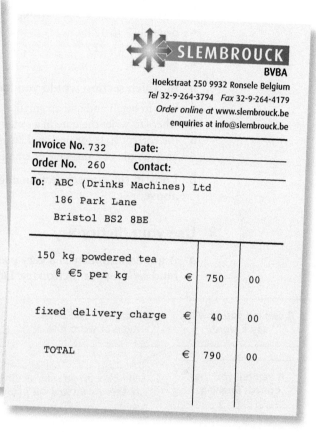

SLEMBROUCK
BVBA
Hoekstraat 250 9932 Ronsele Belgium
Tel 32-9-264-3794 Fax 32-9-264-4179
Order online at www.slembrouck.be
enquiries at info@slembrouck.be

Invoice No. 732	Date:	
Order No. 260	Contact:	

To: ABC (Drinks Machines) Ltd
     186 Park Lane
     Bristol BS2 8BE

150 kg powdered tea @ €5 per kg	€	750	00
fixed delivery charge	€	40	00
TOTAL	€	790	00

3 Slembrouck BVBA have now delivered the orders to the Court Hotel and ABC (Drinks Machines) Ltd. Unfortunately, there are some problems with both orders. In three groups, write the messages between the three companies. The role cards at the back of the book will help you, but you must decide what to write. When you have written your message, 'send' it to the correct group. Then ask for a new card number. (There are three cards for each company.)

Group 1

SLEMBROUCK
BVBA
info@slembrouck.be
Start on card 61

Group 2

THE COURT HOTEL
manager@courthotel.co.uk
Start on card 2

Group 3

ABC
(DRINKS MACHINES) LTD
abc@abcdrinks.com
Start on card 30

1C The writing process   Getting help

1 Use *Company to Company*

There are three sections at the back of the *Company to Company* that can help you while you are writing. What are they? Look at these pages:

- pages 117 to 121
- pages 124 to 127
- page 128

a In which section would you look if you wanted to find the following?

1 how to begin and end an email
2 where to write the date in a letter
3 the correct style for personal business letters
4 an example of a message or email asking for a refund

b Look in the correct section and find the page reference for each item 1–4 above.

2 Use your dictionary

a A good dictionary is a very useful tool when you are writing. You need one! Find *sell* in your dictionary. Does it have this kind of information?

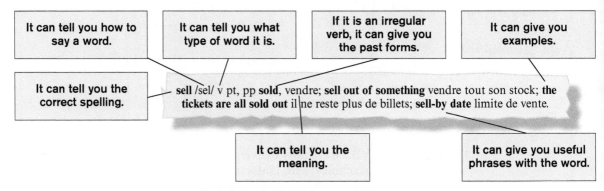

It can tell you how to say a word.

It can tell you what type of word it is.

If it is an irregular verb, it can give you the past forms.

It can give you examples.

It can tell you the correct spelling.

sell /sel/ v pt, pp **sold**, vendre; **sell out of something** vendre tout son stock; **the tickets are all sold out** il ne reste plus de billets; **sell-by date** limite de vente.

It can tell you the meaning.

It can give you useful phrases with the word.

b Sometimes, words have different meanings if you use them as a noun or as a verb. Find these words in your dictionary. What differences in the noun and verb meanings are there?

service   share   credit   trip

c Some words have different spellings in British and American English, or a completely different word is used. Look in your dictionary and complete the tables.

Spelling		Vocabulary	
British English	American English	British English	American English
catalogue	1	note (*money*)	4 ....
2	center	5	apartment
3	check (*money*)	car park	6 ....

Unit 2 Business prospects

2A Study section

- attachments
- parts of a message
- beginning and ending a message
- email conventions

Test yourself

You work for Water Sports Ltd. A woman telephoned your company and asked if you stock Seaworld boat engines and accessories. She was particularly interested in the Wave 78 engine. You said you would send her an email with some brochures about Seaworld engines and tell her when the Seaworld agent is coming to your shop. Write that email. (Invent any details you need.)

When you have finished, put the message away until the end of this section.

2.1 Interfon look for new agents

Interfon, Inc., Japan, are looking for new business, so they sent this email to an international bank in Bahrain. They received the reply shown on page 18.

a Why has Takayuki Aoyama written to Eastern Bank?
b What has Husain Dhaif done with the attached catalogue?

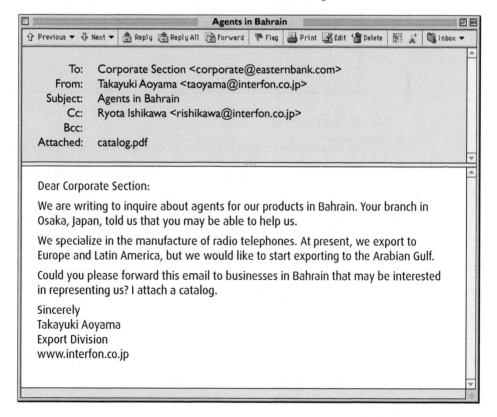

> **Agents in Bahrain**
>
> ⇧ Previous ▼ ⇩ Next ▼ | 📇 Reply 📇 Reply All 📇 Forward | 🚩 Flag | 🖨 Print 📝 Edit 🗑 Delete | 📇 A | 📇 Inbox ▼
>
> **To:** Corporate Section <corporate@easternbank.com>
> **From:** Takayuki Aoyama <taoyama@interfon.co.jp>
> **Subject:** Agents in Bahrain
> **Cc:** Ryota Ishikawa <rishikawa@interfon.co.jp>
> **Bcc:**
> **Attached:** catalog.pdf
>
> Dear Corporate Section:
>
> We are writing to inquire about agents for our products in Bahrain. Your branch in Osaka, Japan, told us that you may be able to help us.
>
> We specialize in the manufacture of radio telephones. At present, we export to Europe and Latin America, but we would like to start exporting to the Arabian Gulf.
>
> Could you please forward this email to businesses in Bahrain that may be interested in representing us? I attach a catalog.
>
> Sincerely
> Takayuki Aoyama
> Export Division
> www.interfon.co.jp

Note that Mr Aoyama is using American English spelling and expressions.
These are covered in more detail in Unit 3.

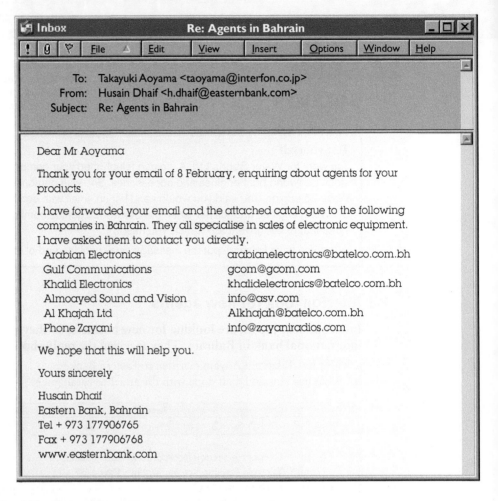

2.2 Attachments

As you saw in Unit 1, if you want to send a file with your email, you can say:

> I am attaching our catalogue to this message. Please contact me if you would
>   like more information.
> Please find attached our report. I look forward to hearing your comments.
> I have just received the photographs, which I have attached to this message.
>   Please can you select the photographs you would like in the newsletter?
> If you have any problems opening the file, please let me know.

Sometimes, people have problems with attachments.

> Thank you for your email. I am afraid you forgot to attach the report. Could you
>   send your message again, please?
> Thank you for your message. Unfortunately, the attachment won't open on my
>   computer. Could you send it again in a different format?
> Sorry! I forgot to send the attachment.

What would you reply to these messages?

a Thank you for your email. I can't find an attachment, however. Did you send it?

b Many thanks for your message. Unfortunately, when I try to open the attachment, my computer crashes.

c Thank you for your reply. Please can you check that you have sent the correct file to me? I requested a copy of your brochure for the DF434 digital camera, but I think you have sent me photographs of your office party.

d I am away from the office for three weeks, so I will not see the report until I get back. Can you send me a copy as an attachment?

e Please find attached an application form for the conference. Please complete it in your word processor and send it back to me.

2.3 Arabian Electronics reply

Some time later, Interfon received this message from Arabian Electronics. Mr Aoyama wrote back straight away.

a What did Arabian Electronics want to know, and what was Interfon's answer?

b Did Mr Aoyama attach details of their products?

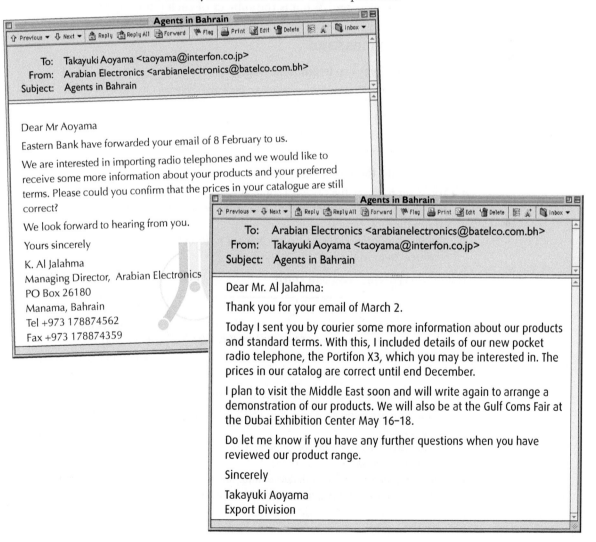

Agents in Bahrain

To: Takayuki Aoyama <taoyama@interfon.co.jp>
From: Arabian Electronics <arabianelectronics@batelco.com.bh>
Subject: Agents in Bahrain

Dear Mr Aoyama

Eastern Bank have forwarded your email of 8 February to us.

We are interested in importing radio telephones and we would like to receive some more information about your products and your preferred terms. Please could you confirm that the prices in your catalogue are still correct?

We look forward to hearing from you.

Yours sincerely

K. Al Jalahma
Managing Director, Arabian Electronics
PO Box 26180
Manama, Bahrain
Tel +973 178874562
Fax +973 178874359

Agents in Bahrain

To: Arabian Electronics <arabianelectronics@batelco.com.bh>
From: Takayuki Aoyama <taoyama@interfon.co.jp>
Subject: Agents in Bahrain

Dear Mr. Al Jalahma:

Thank you for your email of March 2.

Today I sent you by courier some more information about our products and standard terms. With this, I included details of our new pocket radio telephone, the Portifon X3, which you may be interested in. The prices in our catalog are correct until end December.

I plan to visit the Middle East soon and will write again to arrange a demonstration of our products. We will also be at the Gulf Coms Fair at the Dubai Exhibition Center May 16–18.

Do let me know if you have any further questions when you have reviewed our product range.

Sincerely

Takayuki Aoyama
Export Division

2.4 Parts of a message

Most messages have three parts.

> Dear …
> 1 *An opening*
>   This says why you are writing.
> 2 *The main message*
>   This gives the details.
> 3 *The close*
>   This usually talks about the future.
> Yours faithfully/sincerely, etc.

1 Look back at 2.1 and 2.3. Find the three parts in each message. Each part is usually a separate paragraph, but the main message can have more than one paragraph if you are writing about more than one subject.

2 Look at 2.1 and 2.3 again. Which messages have more than one paragraph in the main message? What is the subject of each paragraph?

2.5 Beginning a message

Here are some ways to begin a message.

> We are writing to enquire about …
> We are writing in connection with …
> We are interested in … and we would like to know …

1 How would these messages start?

a You want to know the prices of some air conditioners.
b You saw an advertisement in the newspaper yesterday and you want further information.
c You want to know if the company you are writing to organises business conferences in Malaysia.

If you are replying, you can start:

Thank you for your email/letter/fax/call of (*date*) We have received your email/letter/fax/call of (*date*)	asking if … enquiring about … enclosing … concerning …

2 How would you start your reply in these situations?

a A company sent you an email you on 23 July. They want to know if you sell photocopiers.
b A company sent you a fax on 3 June. They want to know if you are going to a sales exhibition in London.
c A woman telephoned you this morning. She wants to know if your shop is interested in distributing their range of musical instruments.

2.6 Ending a message

Here are some ways to end a message.

> I look forward to receiving your reply/order/products/etc.
> Looking forward to hearing from you.

If you gave some information in your message, you can close:

I hope that this information will help you.	
Please contact me	
Please feel free to contact me	if you need any further information.
Please let me know	

2.7 Practice

Below are the main messages from three emails. Choose the correct beginning and ending from sentences a–f and then add *Yours faithfully/sincerely* or *Best wishes*.

a   Thank you for your telephone call today enquiring about our prices.
b   Thank you for your letter of 16 February concerning Arabian Electronics.
c   I look forward to receiving your order.
d   Thank you for your telephone call today.
e   I hope that this information will help you.
f   Please feel free to contact me if you need any information about other branches.

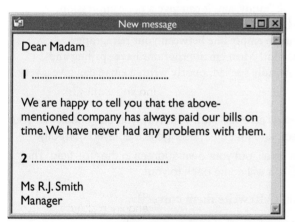

New message

Dear Madam

1 ....

We are happy to tell you that the above-mentioned company has always paid our bills on time. We have never had any problems with them.

2 ....

Ms R.J. Smith
Manager

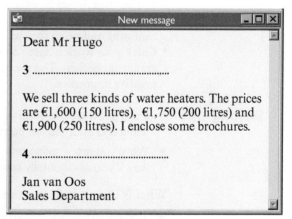

New message

Dear Mr Hugo

3 ....

We sell three kinds of water heaters. The prices are €1,600 (150 litres), €1,750 (200 litres) and €1,900 (250 litres). I enclose some brochures.

4 ....

Jan van Oos
Sales Department

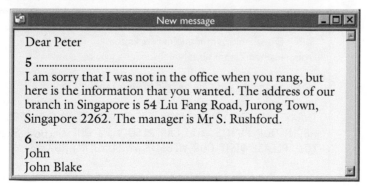

New message

Dear Peter

5 ....
I am sorry that I was not in the office when you rang, but here is the information that you wanted. The address of our branch in Singapore is 54 Liu Fang Road, Jurong Town, Singapore 2262. The manager is Mr S. Rushford.

6 ....
John
John Blake

2.8 Email conventions

Although emails often have an informal style, there are some conventions that you should follow.

- Make sure your emails always open (*Dear ...*) and close properly (*Yours ...*). This is not only polite, it also tells the reader that the message is for them, and not just a copy (cc or bcc), and that the message has finished.
- Don't write in CAPITALS. In email, capitals are the same as shouting! Similarly, don't write all in lower case.
- If you are writing a reply to an email, don't copy the original message back to the person who sent it, unless it is important to do so. However, make it clear what you are replying to. The person you are replying to will normally have a copy of their original message.
- Some email writers copy parts of the original message back to the addressee and then write their reply. Usually, the part that is copied has > in front of it. For example:

```
Create message                                    _ □ ×

Mail to:  Vincenzo Pellegrini <vpellegrini@italialink.it>
Subject:  Re. Distributor details

Dear Mr Pellegrini

> Could you tell me details of your distributors in Italy?
Our main distributor in Italy is Mazzerini Stock House, via Cavour 123, Milano.
```

In general, try to avoid doing this, for the reasons given above. Many users of email also feel this makes an email look untidy, and it can give a poor impression.
- Divide your message into paragraphs. A long message in a single paragraph is confusing and tiring to read. Put an empty line between your paragraphs.
- Check your work before you send it! Most email programs have spelling and grammar checkers. Use them! A badly spelled, poorly written email can give a very negative impression.

Writing tips
- It is a good idea to send yourself an email first. That way, you can check that your name and address are correct, and that the message is displayed correctly.
- While you are working on an email, put your own address in the 'To:' field. That way, if you accidentally send it, it will come back to you!

What is wrong with these emails? Rewrite them correctly.

```
a    Create message                                    _ □ ×

To:    Diana Smith <dsmith@networks.com>
From:  Hamed Zayani <h.zayani@sunderlandpaints.com>

>Please can you send me details of your range of paints and painting
equipment.
THANK YOU FOR YOUR EMAIL. I'VE PUT SOME INFO IN POST TO YOU
ABOUT OUR PIANTS. YOU CAN ALSO VISIT ONE OF OUR SHOPS NEAR
YOU. PLEASE VISIT OUR WEBSITE WW.SUNDERLAND.COM.
```

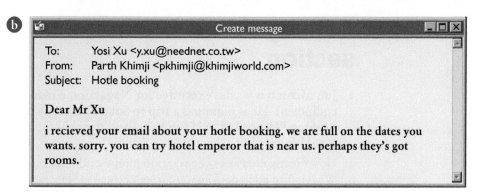

To: Yosi Xu <y.xu@neednet.co.tw>
From: Parth Khimji <pkhimji@khimjiworld.com>
Subject: Hotle booking

Dear Mr Xu

i recieved your email about your hotle booking. we are full on the dates you wants. sorry. you can try hotel emperor that is near us. perhaps they's got rooms.

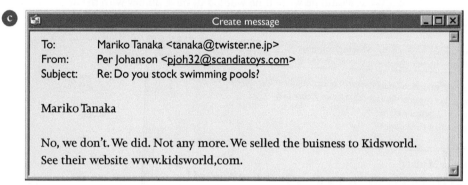

To: Mariko Tanaka <tanaka@twister.ne.jp>
From: Per Johanson <pjoh32@scandiatoys.com>
Subject: Re: Do you stock swimming pools?

Mariko Tanaka

No, we don't. We did. Not any more. We selled the buisness to Kidsworld. See their website www.kidsworld,com.

2.9 Consolidation: a complete email

You work for Hudson Motors Ltd. Last week, a man called Stefan Polloni telephoned you and asked you to send him details of the Sodiac 456 and Sodiac 456i sports cars by email. He has just telephoned to say that he could not open the files you sent. He also wants to know when the two cars will be available (six months from now) and what financing arrangements you offer (special offer now: interest-free for one year, then 5% a year).

Write your message to Stefan Polloni, with the files he needs. First, make a plan for your message. Then compare it with the plan on page 122 before you write your email.

> What have you learned?
> Look back at the message you wrote about Seaworld engines at the beginning of this section. Compare it with your message to Mr Polloni. Can you see an improvement?
> Think about:
> - email conventions
> - subject headings
> - opening/closing a email
> - beginning/ending a message
> - sending attachments.

2B Activity section   A business trip

1 Jun Mizuno is a sales executive for Nagakura, a manufacturer of electrical equipment. He is planning a trip to South-East Asia and wants to visit Leefung Plastics Ltd in Hong Kong and their subsidiary in Singapore. Read his emails.

a How exactly does he say he wants to meet the addressees?
b What information does he want from Leefung in Singapore? How does he ask?
c What would he write if he wanted to have dinner with the addressee?
d What would he write if he wanted to know the name of a good hotel?

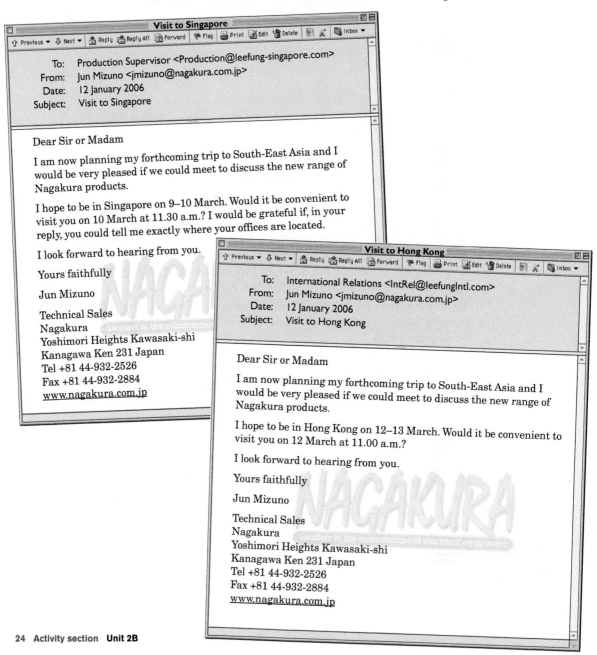

Visit to Singapore

⇧ Previous ▾ ⇩ Next ▾   🖹 Reply 🖹 Reply All 🖹 Forward   🏳 Flag   🖨 Print 🖉 Edit 🗑 Delete   🖵 A⁺   📑 Inbox ▾

To: Production Supervisor <Production@leefung-singapore.com>
From: Jun Mizuno <jmizuno@nagakura.com.jp>
Date: 12 January 2006
Subject: Visit to Singapore

Dear Sir or Madam

I am now planning my forthcoming trip to South-East Asia and I would be very pleased if we could meet to discuss the new range of Nagakura products.

I hope to be in Singapore on 9–10 March. Would it be convenient to visit you on 10 March at 11.30 a.m.? I would be grateful if, in your reply, you could tell me exactly where your offices are located.

I look forward to hearing from you.

Yours faithfully

Jun Mizuno

Technical Sales
Nagakura
Yoshimori Heights Kawasaki-shi
Kanagawa Ken 231 Japan
Tel +81 44-932-2526
Fax +81 44-932-2884
www.nagakura.com.jp

Visit to Hong Kong

⇧ Previous ▾ ⇩ Next ▾   🖹 Reply 🖹 Reply All 🖹 Forward   🏳 Flag   🖨 Print 🖉 Edit 🗑 Delete   🖵 A⁺   📑 Inbox ▾

To: International Relations <IntRel@leefungIntl.com>
From: Jun Mizuno <jmizuno@nagakura.com.jp>
Date: 12 January 2006
Subject: Visit to Hong Kong

Dear Sir or Madam

I am now planning my forthcoming trip to South-East Asia and I would be very pleased if we could meet to discuss the new range of Nagakura products.

I hope to be in Hong Kong on 12–13 March. Would it be convenient to visit you on 12 March at 11.00 a.m.?

I look forward to hearing from you.

Yours faithfully

Jun Mizuno

Technical Sales
Nagakura
Yoshimori Heights Kawasaki-shi
Kanagawa Ken 231 Japan
Tel +81 44-932-2526
Fax +81 44-932-2884
www.nagakura.com.jp

2 After he had sent the email to Leefung Plastics in Hong Kong, Jun Mizuno remembered that he needed some more information, so he sent another email. How does he mention the email he has already sent?

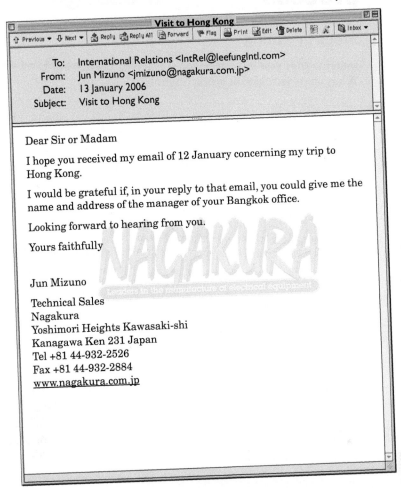

3 Jun Mizuno is now waiting for replies from Leefung Plastics in Hong Kong and in Singapore. In three groups, write the correspondence between them. The role cards at the back of the book will give you some information, but you must decide exactly what to write. Remember to write neat, clear emails, showing names, dates and subject headings. When you have written an email, 'send' it to the correct group. Then ask for a new card number. (There are three cards for each company.)

Group 1	Group 2	Group 3

jmizuno@nagakura.com.jp	IntRel@leefungIntl.com	Production@leefung-singapore.com
Start on card 62	**Start on card 27**	**Start on card 3**

2C The writing process   Steps in writing a message

1 Steps in writing

Imagine that you have received this letter. How would you write a reply?
What steps would you go through?

The Student's Guide

45 Windsor Street
Langford LG56 7HP
England

2 March 2006

Dear Sir or Madam

We are writing to ask if you can help us. We are producing a guide to help students choose
the right job. We would like you to write to us and describe a 'typical day' in your job.

If you are willing to do this, we would be grateful if you could cover the following points in
your reply:
– what exactly you do in your job
– what you like about it
– what you don't like about it
– what you need to be good at the job.

We look forward to hearing from you. Many thanks.

Yours faithfully

Margaret Smith

Margaret Smith
Editor, The Student's Guide
Email: msmith@theguide.org

Work with a partner. Copy the 'cards' below on to separate pieces of paper.
Discuss with your partner the order that you think they go in. You can add any
other cards that you need. When you are ready, stick your cards on to a piece
of paper. Draw arrows to show the order. Compare diagrams with other
students in the class.

Produce a final version.	Send your message!	Check spelling, grammar, style and layout.
Make changes and corrections.	Read carefully the letter you have received.	Make a plan for your message.
Write a draft.	Note down important/ useful phrases.	Read the letter again.

2 Try it out!

Read the letter again. Follow your diagram and write a reply. You can invent
any details you need.

Unit 3 Contacting customers

3A Study section

- referring
- giving good/bad news
- saying what you can/cannot do
- giving reasons
- British and American English
- paragraphs

Test yourself

You work for Conferences Unlimited, a company which arranges conferences. Unfortunately, your office has made a double booking. IBN Computers have booked a conference for 2,000 people, and SJ Finance have booked a conference for 750 people on the same date. Write two emails: one to IBN Computers to confirm their booking and one to SJ Finance to cancel their booking. (Invent any details you need.)

When you have finished, put the message away until the end of this section.

3.1 Giving news

Read the messages on this page and page 28. What do the writers say when they want to:

a refer to the last time that they contacted each other?
b give some good or bad news?
c give a reason for good/bad news?

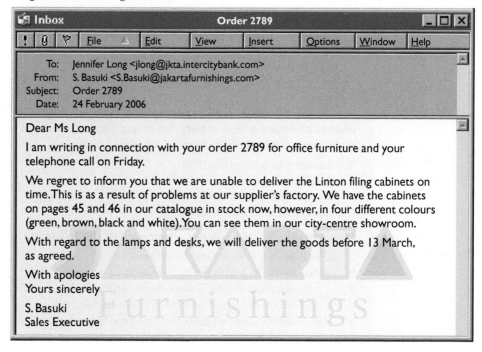

	Inbox	Order 2789	_ □ ✕
!	File Edit View Insert Options Window Help		

To: Jennifer Long <jlong@jkta.intercitybank.com>
From: S. Basuki <S.Basuki@jakartafurnishings.com>
Subject: Order 2789
Date: 24 February 2006

Dear Ms Long

I am writing in connection with your order 2789 for office furniture and your telephone call on Friday.

We regret to inform you that we are unable to deliver the Linton filing cabinets on time. This is as a result of problems at our supplier's factory. We have the cabinets on pages 45 and 46 in our catalogue in stock now, however, in four different colours (green, brown, black and white). You can see them in our city-centre showroom.

With regard to the lamps and desks, we will deliver the goods before 13 March, as agreed.

With apologies
Yours sincerely

S. Basuki
Sales Executive

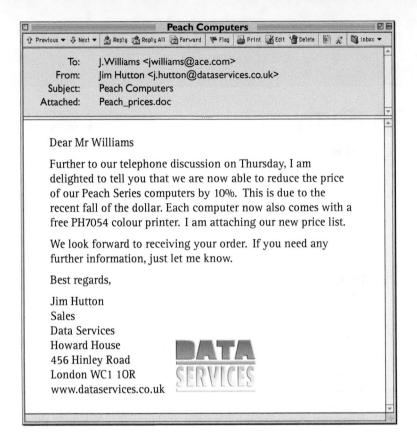

To: J.Williams <jwilliams@ace.com>
From: Jim Hutton <j.hutton@dataservices.co.uk>
Subject: Peach Computers
Attached: Peach_prices.doc

Dear Mr Williams

Further to our telephone discussion on Thursday, I am delighted to tell you that we are now able to reduce the price of our Peach Series computers by 10%. This is due to the recent fall of the dollar. Each computer now also comes with a free PH7054 colour printer. I am attaching our new price list.

We look forward to receiving your order. If you need any further information, just let me know.

Best regards,

Jim Hutton
Sales
Data Services
Howard House
456 Hinley Road
London WC1 1OR
www.dataservices.co.uk

3.2 Referring

Here are some ways to introduce the subject of the message.

> With reference to ...
> Further to ...
> I am writing in connection with ...
> With regard to ...

Writing tip You should not usually start a letter or email with *with regard to*. This phrase is not used to introduce a topic initially, but to add information about another aspect of a topic. Look at the message from Jakarta Furnishings in 3.1.

You can refer to a topic like this:
  Dear Ms Jenkins
  Re: invoice 14673
Re: stands for *with reference to*.

How would you start a letter about each of the following?

a   an invoice (no. 679) for a photocopier
b   a meeting you had with the addressee on 16 January
c   an advertisement in *The Times* newspaper for the London Trade Fair
d   an application for a post as secretary in your company
e   a fax order for six computers that you received today

3.3 Giving good/bad news

good news

I am	pleased delighted happy	to	tell inform advise	you that …

bad news

We/I	regret are/am sorry	to	tell inform advise	you that …
We regret that …				

Writing tip Writers often say 'we' to refer to the company, rather than 'I'. This is especially true when giving bad news, as it makes it less personal.

Complete these sentences using phrases for referring and giving good or bad news.

a .... your order for some cupboards, ... we have had to increase the price.

b .... your application for a post as secretary, ... that we would like you to start work as soon as possible.

c .... your application for a post as secretary; .... you were not successful.

d .... our telephone conversation last week, ... that your car is now ready for you to collect.

3.4 Saying what you can and cannot do

| We are unable to … |
| We are able to … |
| We have been forced to … |

A company has written to you to ask you to reduce your prices and to ask you if you will accept payment in Egyptian pounds. How will you give them the following information?

a You cannot lower your prices.

b You have had to raise your prices because the government has increased the sales tax.

c However, you can give them a discount of 5% if their order is for more than $8,000 or €8,000.

d With regard to their second question, you cannot accept payment in Egyptian pounds, but you can accept US dollars or euros.

3.5 Giving reasons

This is	owing to …
	due to …
	as a result of …
	because of …

Writing tips

- *Owing to* is normally only used for bad news.
- If you want to use a verb after these phrases, add *the fact that …*, e.g. *This is due to the fact that the dollar has risen.*
- If you don't want to give the reason, you can say *unforeseen circumstances* or *factors beyond our control*, e.g. *This is due to unforeseen circumstances. This is as a result of factors beyond our control.*

Use the phrases from 3.4 and 3.5 and the information below to write complete sentences as in the example. Be careful with e and f (see *Writing tips*).

a increase – fall of the dollar
   We have been forced to increase our prices. This is owing to the fall of the dollar.
b delay the delivery of the goods – strike by airline pilots
c increase all salaries by 10% – rise in sales
d cut all salaries by 10% – fall in sales
e cannot deliver your new order – we have not received your payment for the last order
f cancel the meeting – a lot of staff have been ill

3.6 An American English writer

There are some differences between American and British English.
Compare this email with the emails in 3.1. What differences can you see?

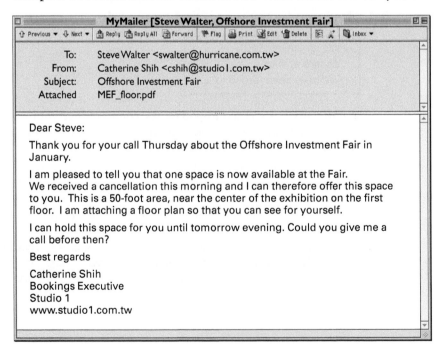

MyMailer [Steve Walter, Offshore Investment Fair]

⇧ Previous ▼ ⬇ Next ▼ | 🖹 Reply 🖹 Reply All 🖹 Forward | 🏳 Flag | 🖨 Print 🖹 Edit 🗑 Delete | 🖹 A' | 📥 Inbox ▼

To: Steve Walter <swalter@hurricane.com.tw>
From: Catherine Shih <cshih@studio1.com.tw>
Subject: Offshore Investment Fair
Attached   MEF_floor.pdf

Dear Steve:

Thank you for your call Thursday about the Offshore Investment Fair in January.

I am pleased to tell you that one space is now available at the Fair.
We received a cancellation this morning and I can therefore offer this space to you. This is a 50-foot area, near the center of the exhibition on the first floor. I am attaching a floor plan so that you can see for yourself.

I can hold this space for you until tomorrow evening. Could you give me a call before then?

Best regards

Catherine Shih
Bookings Executive
Studio 1
www.studio1.com.tw

3.7 British and American English

The main difference between British English (BE) and American English (AE) is accent, but you do not need to worry about that when you are writing! There are, however, some important differences in written forms.

Style

AE writers often use a more informal style than BE. For example, an AE writer may open a letter *Dear Steven* where a BE writer would open with *Dear Mr Brown* unless he/she knows the person well.

If an AE writer does not know the person's name, they may use the job title – *Dear Corporate Section Manager:* – where a BE writer would write *Dear Sir or Madam*. Notice the colon (:) which AE writers sometimes use after the opening.

Spelling

-re in BE is often *-er* in AE: *centre/center, theatre/theater, metre/meter*
-our in BE is often *-or* in AE: *colour/color, favourite/favorite, labour/labor*
-se in BE is often *-ze* in AE: *analyse/analyze, criticise/criticize, recognise/recognize*
-ogue in BE is often *-og* in AE: *catalogue/catalog, dialogue/dialog*

Vocabulary

There are many vocabulary differences between BE and AE. For example:

British English	American English
curriculum vitae	résumé
note (*money*)	bill
bill (*in a restaurant*)	check
ground floor	first floor
petrol	gas
postcode	zip code
property	real estate
shop	store
city/town centre	downtown
mobile phone	cell phone

Grammar

AE usually uses the past simple where BE uses the present perfect. For example:
BE   *I have spoken to Per about this. Have you asked Margareta?*
AE   *I spoke to Per about this. Did you ask Margareta?*

Writing tip You can use British English or American English. The most important point is that you are consistent, or it will look like a mistake. For example, do not write *You can see the different colours in our catalog*. Write *colours* and *catalogue*, or *colors* and *catalog*. Check in a dictionary if you are not sure.

1 **Are these examples of British or American English? Change them into American/British English.**

a You'll find our offices on the ground floor.
b Please send us a copy of your résumé.
c The theater is downtown, next to a large store.
d Please give your name, address and postcode, and we will send you a catalogue.
e We specialize in downtown real estate.

2 **Correct the errors in this advert. Make it fully American or British.**

WE STOCK AN AMAZING SELECTION OF STYLES AND COLORS, ALL AT A PRICE THAT YOU'LL FIND HARD TO BEAT. WE'RE SURE TO HAVE YOUR FAVORITE. ON OUR GROUND FLOOR, YOU'LL FIND A WIDE RANGE OF FURNITURE FOR YOUR HOME. ON OUR FIRST FLOOR, WE HAVE SPECIAL DEALS ON OFFICE FURNITURE.

VISIT BROWN'S FURNITURE SHOP: NEAR THE ENZO GAS STATION, IN THE CITY CENTRE.
SEND US YOUR NAME, ADDRESS AND ZIP CODE FOR OUR NEW CATALOGUE. *FREE!*

3.8 Paragraphs

Most messages are divided into paragraphs. A paragraph can have just one sentence in it, or it can have many sentences. The most important point is that a paragraph should have one central topic.

1 Look at the messages in 2.1, 2.3, 3.1 and 3.6 (pages 17–19, 27–28 and 30). What is the topic of each paragraph?

2 Divide these two messages into separate paragraphs. How many paragraphs do you need? Are the messages in British or American English?

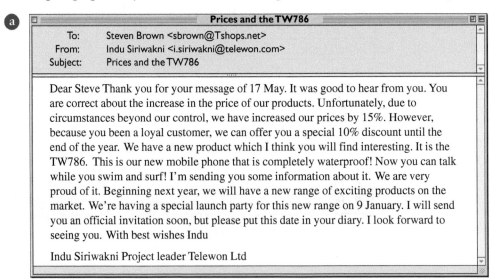

a

> **Prices and the TW786**
>
> To: Steven Brown <sbrown@Tshops.net>
> From: Indu Siriwakni <i.siriwakni@telewon.com>
> Subject: Prices and the TW786
>
> Dear Steve Thank you for your message of 17 May. It was good to hear from you. You are correct about the increase in the price of our products. Unfortunately, due to circumstances beyond our control, we have increased our prices by 15%. However, because you been a loyal customer, we can offer you a special 10% discount until the end of the year. We have a new product which I think you will find interesting. It is the TW786. This is our new mobile phone that is completely waterproof! Now you can talk while you swim and surf! I'm sending you some information about it. We are very proud of it. Beginning next year, we will have a new range of exciting products on the market. We're having a special launch party for this new range on 9 January. I will send you an official invitation soon, but please put this date in your diary. I look forward to seeing you. With best wishes Indu
>
> Indu Siriwakni Project leader Telewon Ltd

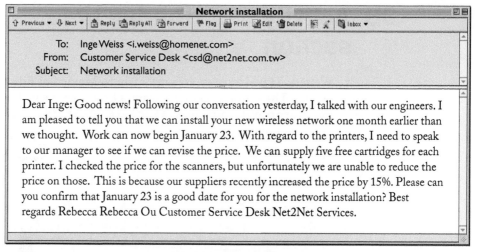

Network installation

⇧ Previous ▾   ⬇ Next ▾   Reply   Reply All   Forward   Flag   Print   Edit   Delete   A'   Inbox ▾

To: Inge Weiss <i.weiss@homenet.com>
From: Customer Service Desk <csd@net2net.com.tw>
Subject: Network installation

Dear Inge: Good news! Following our conversation yesterday, I talked with our engineers. I am pleased to tell you that we can install your new wireless network one month earlier than we thought. Work can now begin January 23. With regard to the printers, I need to speak to our manager to see if we can revise the price. We can supply five free cartridges for each printer. I checked the price for the scanners, but unfortunately we are unable to reduce the price on those. This is because our suppliers recently increased the price by 15%. Please can you confirm that January 23 is a good date for you for the network installation? Best regards Rebecca Rebecca Ou Customer Service Desk Net2Net Services.

3 **How many paragraphs do you need for each of these messages?**
What would you say in each paragraph?

a   You have to write to all your customers, telling them that your office has moved.
b   You have to write to all your customers, telling them that your manager has left and that a new woman now has the job. You can tell them something about where she has come from and what her experience is.
c   You work in a car motor supplies company. A customer has written to complain about your service, your prices and the low quality of your products. You have to write back, apologising for the customer's bad experience and explaining what went wrong in each case. You can give the customer a €500 credit as compensation.

3.9 Consolidation: a complete email

You are the sub-manager of a bank. There has been a change in government regulations. Interest rates have increased to 12% for deposits and 14% for loans. Write short messages to:

a   customers who have deposit accounts with you
b   customers who have a loan from you.

First make a plan for each message. Then compare your plans with the one on page 122 before you write the messages.

What have you learned?
Look back at the messages you wrote to IBN Computers and SJ Finance at the beginning of this section. Compare it with your messages to the bank customers in 3.9. Can you see an improvement? Think about:
● introducing the subject
● giving good/bad news
● giving reasons
● AE or BE style
● paragraphs.

3B Activity section   Holiday time

1 Western Travel have to arrange a trip to Mexico in July for a group of 25 people. The group organisers want a tour with a small company, not one of the larger travel companies. They have selected two tours, but want to keep the costs down.

a Which company is cheaper if the group is travelling in July and wants twin-bedded rooms and insurance?

b Do both companies use the same airline?

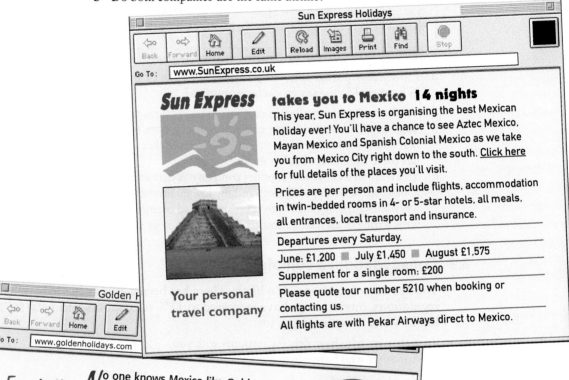

Sun Express Holidays

Go To: www.SunExpress.co.uk

Sun Express takes you to Mexico **14 nights**

This year, Sun Express is organising the best Mexican holiday ever! You'll have a chance to see Aztec Mexico, Mayan Mexico and Spanish Colonial Mexico as we take you from Mexico City right down to the south. Click here for full details of the places you'll visit.

Prices are per person and include flights, accommodation in twin-bedded rooms in 4- or 5-star hotels, all meals, all entrances, local transport and insurance.

Departures every Saturday.

June: £1,200 ■ July £1,450 ■ August £1,575

Supplement for a single room: £200

Please quote tour number 5210 when booking or contacting us.

All flights are with Pekar Airways direct to Mexico.

Your personal travel company

Golden H

Go To: www.goldenholidays.com

Experience Mexico with

Golden Holidays

No one knows Mexico like Golden Holidays!
Come with us on our tour of this fabulous country and you'll see sights you've never dreamed of ... the Mayan pyramids of Palenque, Chichen-Itza and Uxma ... the sparkling water and white sands of the Caribbean ... the exciting atmosphere of Acapulco ... and much, much more!

Price: £1,300 per person, including flights, all meals and all excursions for 15 days. Price is based on two people sharing a twin-bedded room.

Supplement for a single room: £175

Insurance available at £75 per person

Carrier: Stanley Air

Departures every Tuesday in June, July and August.

Special discounts for groups of more than 30: 12%

2 Western Travel called Sun Express to ask them if they could offer a group discount. They received this email. Which company is cheaper now?

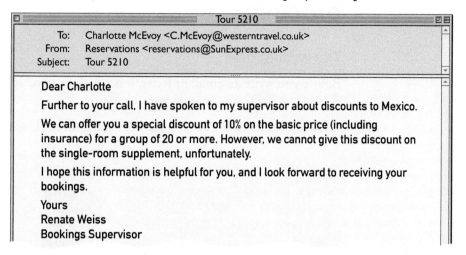

Tour 5210

To: Charlotte McEvoy <C.McEvoy@westerntravel.co.uk>
From: Reservations <reservations@SunExpress.co.uk>
Subject: Tour 5210

Dear Charlotte

Further to your call, I have spoken to my supervisor about discounts to Mexico.

We can offer you a special discount of 10% on the basic price (including insurance) for a group of 20 or more. However, we cannot give this discount on the single-room supplement, unfortunately.

I hope this information is helpful for you, and I look forward to receiving your bookings.

Yours
Renate Weiss
Bookings Supervisor

3 As Sun Express were now cheaper than Golden Holidays, Western Travel made the bookings with Sun Express.

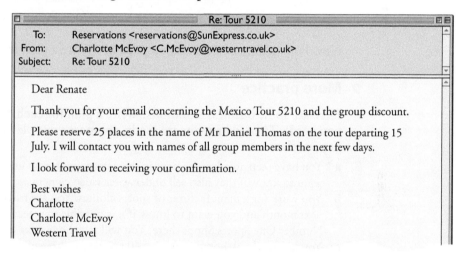

Re: Tour 5210

To: Reservations <reservations@SunExpress.co.uk>
From: Charlotte McEvoy <C.McEvoy@westerntravel.co.uk>
Subject: Re: Tour 5210

Dear Renate

Thank you for your email concerning the Mexico Tour 5210 and the group discount.

Please reserve 25 places in the name of Mr Daniel Thomas on the tour departing 15 July. I will contact you with names of all group members in the next few days.

I look forward to receiving your confirmation.

Best wishes
Charlotte
Charlotte McEvoy
Western Travel

Western Travel are now waiting to receive confirmation from Sun Express. In three groups, write the correspondence between Western Travel, Sun Express and Golden Holidays. When you have written an email, 'send' it to the correct group. Then ask for a new card number. (There are three cards for each group.)

Group 1

reservations@SunExpress.co.uk
Start on card 54

Group 2

reservations@goldenholidays.com
Start on card 31

Group 3

C.McEvoy@westerntravel.co.uk
Start on card 8

3C The writing process

Writing a plan

1 The writing plan

Before you write an email or letter, it is usually a good idea to make a plan. A plan can help you organise your ideas.

Look at the emails in 2.1 on page 17. Match these plans to the correct email.

a

- *Dear ...*
- Open the message. Thank them for their letter.
- Say what you have done. Give the information.
- Close the message.
- *Yours ...*
- Give your name and title.

b

- *Dear ...*
- Open the message. Say why you are writing and who gave you their address.
- Say what you want to do.
- Ask them to help.
- Close the message.
- *Yours ...*
- Give your name and title.

Now look at the emails in 3.1 on page 27. Write a plan for each email.

2 More practice

Here are some business situations. Write a plan for each one (invent any details you need). Then, when you are ready, compare your plans with other students in your class.

a You have seen an advertisement in the newspaper for an underwater camera. You want to know if they also sell underwater video cameras.

b You work for a manufacturer of sports clothes. You are travelling to Los Angeles next month and you want to know if it is possible to meet the managing director of Number One Sports Shops there. You will telephone next week to confirm.

c You have to book hotel rooms for 40 people for three nights. You want to send an email to four different hotels to ask them what they charge.

d This morning you found a message on your answering machine. A woman left an order for 35 boxes of paper towels. She left her name and email address. Unfortunately, your company makes furniture, not paper towels. She telephoned the wrong number. Your number is 273456. The number she needs is 237456.

Unit 4 When things go wrong

4A Study section

- letter layout
- the date
- making mild complaints
- making a point
- warning
- making strong complaints

Test yourself

Six months ago, you sent an invoice to a company, Tiger Transport Ltd. You have reminded them twice, but they have still not paid you. Write a letter (not an email) to them, reminding them again that credit is only available for 30 days, and that if they do not pay, you will take legal action. (Invent any details that you need.)

When you have finished, put the letter away until the end of this section.

4.1 Intercity Bank write to complain

Intercity Bank ordered some office furniture from Jakarta Furnishings (see pages 7 and 27). The filing cabinets did not arrive, so Ms Long wrote to complain. To make her complaint more formal, she decided to write a letter. She received a reply from Mr Basuki. As you read the letters on this page and the next, find the answers to these questions.

a How does Ms Long complain?
b What does Mr Basuki want Ms Long to look at?
c Will Mr Basuki refund the bank's money?

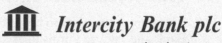

IIII *Intercity Bank plc*

Your ref:
Our ref: JL/fh/246

Jalan Thamin 58
Jakarta 11196
Indonesia
Tel 021 6376008
Fax 021 6376733
www.intercitybank.com/indonesia

Mr S. Basuki
Jakarta Furnishings
Jalan Arjuna 7
Jakarta 11190

30 May 2006

Dear Mr Basuki

Order 2789

I am writing in connection with your email of 24 February concerning the above order for some office furniture.

Unfortunately, we have not yet received the filing cabinets which were a part of this order. We would be grateful if you could deliver these as soon as possible or refund our money.

We look forward to hearing from you.

Yours sincerely

Jennifer Long

Ms Jennifer Long
Office Manager

JAKARTA
Furnishings

Jalan Arjuna 7
Jakarta 11190
Tel 021 6373742
Fax 021 6373739

Ms Jennifer Long
Office Manager
Intercity Bank plc
Jalan Thamin 58
Jakarta 11196

2 June 2006

Your ref: JL/fh/246
Our ref: SB/sl

Dear Ms Long

Order 2789

Thank you for your letter of 30 May enquiring about the Linton filing cabinets.

We must apologise for the delay in delivering these cabinets. As I said in my email of 24 February, this is a result of problems at our supplier's factory. As these problems are completely beyond our control, I should like to point out that we are not able to refund your payment. I enclose a copy of our Terms of Sale for your reference.

We expect to receive the goods next week, so I hope that you will not have to wait much longer.

With apologies once again,

Yours sincerely

S. Basuki
Sales Executive

4.2 Letter layout: block style

There are many ways to lay out a business letter. The letters from Intercity Bank and Jakarta Furnishings are examples of the most common way. Look at the letters and complete the descriptions with the correct words from the box.

> top   bottom   right   left   after   under

a   The address of the sender (the person who is writing) is at the .... , on the ....

b   The name and address of the addressee (the person you are writing to) is at the .... , on the ....

c   The date is at the .... , on the .... , ... the address.

d   The subject heading is .... *Dear …*

e   The paragraphs start at the .... margin. Between the paragraphs, there is a space.

f   The signature is .... *Yours …*

g   The name and title of the sender is at the .... , ... the signature.

h   There is no punctuation in the addresses or .... *Dear …* or .... *Yours faithfully/sincerely.*

4.3 The date

Writing tip Be careful with the date! In British English, they write the day first, but in American English, they write the month first. This means that 12-06-2006 is the twelfth of June in Britain, but in the United States it is the sixth of December! So, write the date like this:

12 June 2006

and then everybody will know what you mean. Remember to use a capital letter for the month. You do not have to write *st*, *nd*, *rd* or *th* after the day.

How would you write these dates in a letter?

a   Jan. 16th, 2006
b   23rd March 2007
c   6/11/08 (UK)
d   09-07-06 (USA)
e   21.1.07
f   04.08.02 (USA)

4.4 Practice

Look at this letter. What's wrong with it? (Look back on what you have learned in Units 1–3.) Write out the letter correctly, in 'block style'.

> Slottsberget 26,
> Goteborg 41803,
> Sweden
> Tel +46 31 274906
>
> Ms Susan Benton
> Island World Holidays
> 181 North Street
> London W1M 2FM
>
> Dear Sir
> I am writing in connection with my booking with you for an adventure holiday to Peru.
> On the nineteenth of May I sent you a cheque for £260 as a deposit. Unfortunately, I have not yet received a receipt for this. I would be grateful if you could send me this as soon as possible.
> I look forward to hearing from you.
>
> 2006, july 21st
> Your ref. PER23/675
> Best wishes
> Margareta Lindell
>
> *Margareta Lindell*

4.5 Making a mild complaint

To make a mild complaint you can say:

> Unfortunately, we have not yet received the filing cabinets.

and then request some action.

Please could you We would be grateful if you could We would appreciate it if you could	deliver them soon.

1 **Match sentences a–d to sentences e–h to make four separate complaints.**

a Unfortunately, one of the machines you sent us was damaged.
b Unfortunately, we have not yet received your payment.
c Unfortunately, your driver took the goods to the wrong place.
d Unfortunately, you forgot to mention the cost of your products.

e Please could you send us your cheque before 30 June?
f We would be grateful if you could send us a replacement.
g We would appreciate it if you could collect them and bring them to our offices.
h Please could you send your price list as soon as possible?

2 **What would you write in these situations? In each case, decide what action you want the company or organisation to take.**

a A company has sent you a bill for the wrong goods.
Unfortunately, you sent us a bill for the wrong goods. Please could you send us the correct bill as soon as possible?
b Your new photocopier has broken down five times in the last week. You have to write to the company who sold it to you.
c Two temporary secretaries do not speak English. You have to write to the agency who sent them to you.
d You keep receiving letters for someone else. You have to write to the post office.

4.6 Letter practice

The accountant in your office has just passed you this invoice and note.

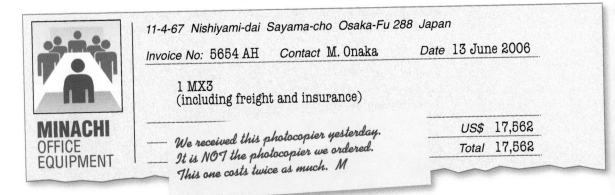

11-4-67 Nishiyami-dai Sayama-cho Osaka-Fu 288 Japan

Invoice No: 5654 AH   Contact M. Onaka   Date 13 June 2006

1 MX3
(including freight and insurance)

MINACHI
OFFICE
EQUIPMENT

We received this photocopier yesterday. It is NOT the photocopier we ordered. This one costs twice as much. M

US$ 17,562
Total 17,562

Write a full letter to Minachi complaining about the photocopier. First, make a plan. Then compare it with the one on page 122 before you write the letter.

4.7 Making a point

If you want someone to take note of something, you can use phrases such as:

> I should like to draw your attention to (the fact that) …
> I should like to point out that …

If you are saying something that they already know (and you are a little bit angry), you can write:

> I should like to remind you that …
> I hope that it is not necessary to remind you that …

You have been passed these messages. What will you write?

a

From: S. Patel
Date: 8/10

Terry Spencer keeps parking his car in front
of the main door.
I have told him before that this space is reserved for the
Managing Director. Can you tell him again?

b

❖ Inter-Office Memo ❖

From: RJR **To:** DA **Date:** 9/10

Muriel McIver arrives half an hour late for work every
day. (She should start at 9.30.)
We now need to give her a written reminder.
Please can you write to her?

c

Steve,
The photocopier has broken down again. Can
you send them an email? This is the third
time it has broken down this month. The last
time, they promised it wouldn't happen again.
                                          A.

4.8 Intercity Bank have to write again

Three months later, Intercity Bank had still not received the filing cabinets. Jennifer Long decided to write again.

a   Is Ms Long still making a mild complaint? How do you know?
b   What will she do if she does not get a reply to her letter?

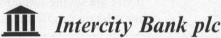

Intercity Bank plc

Your ref:
Our ref: JL/fh/246

Jalan Thamin 58
Jakarta 11196
Indonesia
Tel 021 6376008
Fax 021 6376733
www.intercitybank.com/indonesia

26 August 2006

Mr S. Basuki
Jakarta Furnishings
Jalan Arjuna 7
Jakarta 11190

Dear Mr Basuki

Order 2789

I am writing in connection with the above order for Linton filing cabinets.

It is now over seven months since we placed the order, and we are still waiting for the cabinets. I should like to remind you that we have already paid for these cabinets. We must insist, therefore, that you deliver them immediately or refund our money.

Unless we hear from you within seven days, we will be forced to take legal action.

Yours sincerely

Jennifer Long

Ms Jennifer Long
Office Manager

4.9 Warning

One way to warn somebody is to say:

Unless ... , If ... (not) ... ,	we will be forced to ...

What warnings would you give these people?

a   a company that has not paid your bill
b   another company that is using your company's car park
c   an employee who always arrives late for work
d   a builder who has left a lot of tools in your office

4.10 Making a strong complaint

To make a strong complaint, you can:

- say exactly what is wrong

> It is now over nine months since we placed this order and we are still waiting for the cabinets.

- make a point connected with this

> I should like to point out that we have already paid for these cabinets.

- demand immediate action

> We must insist, therefore, that you deliver them immediately.

If you think that it is necessary, you can also:

- give a warning

> Unless we hear from you within seven days, we will take legal action.

The letters on this page and page 44 are mixed up. Put the sentences in the correct order and divide each one into three paragraphs.

The Manager
Swindle Cleaning Co
City Centre Towers
Winley WY6 7TY

Dear Sir or Madam

a   I hope it is not necessary to remind you that this is the second time I have complained about your employees.

b   If you are unable to do this, we will be forced to cancel your contract with us.

c   I am writing in connection with your contract to clean our offices.

d   I must insist, therefore, that you take immediate action to improve the quality of your services.

e   Twice this week, I have found your workers asleep when they should be working.

Yours faithfully

H.J. Wilson

H.J. Wilson
Senior Administrator

②

Dear Sir or Madam

a   We booked and paid for a quarter-page advertisement on the front page of the Friday edition of your newspaper.

b   I am writing to complain about our advertisement which appeared in your newspaper on 10 July.

c   I would like to remind you that this is the third time that this has happened.

d   If you do not do this, we will be forced to take all our advertising business to one of your competitors.

e   As we are regular advertisers in your newspapers, I must insist that you repeat the advertisement this Saturday, on the front page, free of charge.

f   However, the advertisement did not appear until Saturday, and only on page 4.

Yours faithfully

Daniel Thomas

Mr Daniel Thomas
Public Relations

4.11 Consolidation: a complete letter

You work at Central Business Consultants, 16 Hyde Towers, Hong Kong. The people who rent the offices next to you play very loud music all day, every day, even though the contract says that 'music is not allowed'. It is impossible for you to work.

Write a full letter to them, making a strong complaint. First, make a plan for your letter. Then compare it with the plan on page 122 before you write your letter.

> What have you learned?
> Look back at the letter you wrote to Tiger Transport Ltd at the beginning of this section. Compare it with your letter about the problem with music in 4.11.
> Can you see an improvement? Think about:
> • letter layout
> • the date
> • mild and strong complaints
> • warning.

4B Activity section   Who's responsible?

1 Read this newspaper article about an explosion in a clothes factory and answer these questions.

a How much was Perfecta's stock valued at?
b What are Perfecta going to do now?
c Who are Bauer AG?
d What have Aqua Warm done?

Daily News   *3 January 2006*

Explosion destroys factory

A HUGE explosion caused extensive damage to a multimillion-euro factory last night.

The explosion ripped through the state-of-the-art premises of Perfecta Ltd, the well-known clothes designer. There were no injuries. A spokesman for Perfecta said that the central-heating system had exploded, destroying most of their stock and blasting a hole in the factory roof.

'Our entire spring stock has been destroyed. We have lost close to a million euros worth of clothes,' he said. He claimed that they wrote to Bauer AG, who installed the heating system, on 9 December last year, because of unusual noises in the system. They received no reply. He said Perfecta will be claiming compensation from Bauer AG.

Meanwhile, Perfecta have been forced to close the factory because of the damage and low temperatures. In addition to their stock losses, factory closure will cost them €50,000 a day in lost production, according to the spokesman.

Amsterdam: Aqua Warm BV, the manufacturers of the heating unit, said last night that they have been making central-heating systems for over 25 years with no previous complaints. They have asked a surveyor to report on the Perfecta explosion.

2 Perfecta now want compensation from Bauer AG and also to get the factory working again. In three groups, you must write the correspondence between them. When you have written a letter or an email, 'send' it to the correct group. Then ask for a new card number. (There are three cards for each company.)

Group 1

Start on card 23

Group 2

Start on card 46

Group 3

Start on card 29

4C The writing process

Read before you write

1 Read!

Before you write a reply to a letter, it is best to carefully read the letter you received. This will help your reply. Match the numbers 1–6 to comments a–f.

a   Mention the date.
b   Notice the style (formal/informal).
c   Copy the address carefully.
d   Read the main part of the message carefully.
e   Use subject headings and references.
f   Notice how the writer refers to him/herself.

🏛 Intercity Bank plc

Your ref:
Our ref: JL/fh/246 ❶

Jalan Thamin 58
Jakarta 11196
Indonesia❷
Tel 021 6376008
Fax 021 6376733
www.intercitybank.com/indonesia

Mr S. Basuki
Jakarta Furnishings
Jalan Arjuna 7
Jakarta 11190

26 August 2006❸

Dear Mr Basuki

Order 2789 ❶

I am writing in connection with the above order for Linton filing cabinets. ❹

It is now over seven months since we placed the order, and we are still waiting for the cabinets. I should like to remind you that we have already paid for these cabinets. We must insist, therefore, that you deliver them immediately or refund our money. ❺

Unless we hear from you within seven days, we will be forced to take legal action.

Yours sincerely

Jennifer Long

Ms Jennifer Long ❻
Office Manager

2 A reply

Rewrite this reply, correcting the mistakes.

JAKARTA
Furnishings

Jalan Arjuna 7
Jakarta 11190
Tel 021 6373742
Fax 021 6373739

Ms Jennifer Long
Office Manager
Intercity Bank plc
Jalan Thamin 58
Jakarta 11196

28 August 2006

Your ref: JL/fh/246
Our ref: SB/sl

Dear Jennifer

Thank you for your letter.

I'm sorry you are unhappy with the Linton filing cabinets. I can't refund your money, I'm afraid, as you have had these cabinets for seven months. I don't think there is much point in you taking legal action, as you are unlikely to succeed. We do try to advise customers to get what they need, but the final decision is always the customers.

I am sorry I cannot be of more help.

Yours faithfully

S. Basuki

S. Basuki
Sales Executive

5A Study section

- requesting action
- apologising
- faxes

Test yourself

You work for Sunshine Airways. You have just received a letter from a customer who says she had a terrible flight, that her bags did not arrive until two days later, and that one of her bags was broken. Write a letter to send by fax, apologising and asking for further information so that you can arrange compensation. (Invent any details you need.)

When you have finished, put the letter away until the end of this section.

5.1 Construcciones Jiménez ask about delivery

Construcciones Jiménez SA, Spain, ordered some drills from Haga Verktyg, Sweden. They arranged a letter of credit, but after two months, Haga Verktyg had still not sent the goods. As Construcciones Jiménez wanted to get an immediate reply, they decided to send a fax. As you read their fax and the reply, find the answers to the questions on page 49.

Fax +34 58 345545 13-05-2006 16:04 p.01

FAX COVER SHEET	For the attention of: Export Manager
CONSTRUCCIONES JIMÉNEZ	Organisation: Haga Verktyg, Göteborg, Sweden
Avda del Pueblo Granada España	Fax No. +46 31 638420
Tel/Fax +34 58 345545	Date: 13 May 2006
info@jimenezcons.es	
www.jimenezcons.es	

Dear Sir or Madam

Our order No. 2886: 5 Kraftborr drills

As it is now more than two months since we opened a letter of credit in your favour, we would be grateful if you could arrange shipment of the goods as soon as possible. We would appreciate it if you could let us know exactly when the goods will arrive.

We look forward to receiving the drills.

Yours

José Muñoz

Name: José Muñoz
Title/Department: Manager, Purchasing
No. of pages to follow: 0

a letter of credit (l/c)
a bank paper that guarantees payment **in your favour** *in your name, payable to you*

Your ref:
Our ref: JM/ps/20B

HAGA VERKTYG

Kaponjärgatan 4c
Göteborg 41877
Sweden

Tel: +46 31 453423
Fax: +46 31 638420
hv@hagaverktyg.net.se

José Muñoz,
Manager, Purchasing
Construcciones Jiménez
Avda del Pueblo
Granada
Spain

15 May 2006

Dear Sr Muñoz

Thank you for your fax dated 13 May concerning your order for five drills.

We must apologise for the delay in shipping this order. This was due to unforeseen circumstances. However, we are dealing with your order now, and it will be sent without further delay.

With apologies once again,

Yours sincerely

Mona Stenlund

Mona Stenlund
Export Manager

a   What do Construcciones Jiménez want Haga Verktyg to do?
b   How exactly do Haga Verktyg apologise?
c   Why haven't Haga Verktyg sent the goods?

5.2 Requesting action

Here are some ways to ask people to do something for you.

If it is urgent, add:

Please could you …
We would be grateful
  if you could …
We would appreciate it
  if you could …
	send us …
	arrange …
	give us further details about …
	let us know (about/if) …
	inform us (about/if) …
		as soon as possible.
		without delay.
		immediately.

Writing tip   *Please could you …* is the most direct. You can use this phrase when you are asking for something in a neutral way. The other two phrases are more polite and forceful.

1 **These requests are mixed up. Put the words in the correct order.**

a please / arrange / for ten o'clock / could / an appointment / you
b we / send / as soon as possible / would / if you / the goods / be grateful / could
c we / without delay / appreciate it / you could / pay our bill / would / if
d confirm / please / you / are the same / could / your prices / that
e we / exactly when / appreciate it / if you / would / could / tell us / you will arrive

2 **What would you write in these situations?**

a You sent a message to someone and they haven't replied. You want to know if they received it.
b A businessman is coming to your country. He wants you to get a visa for him. You need his passport details (nationality, date of birth, date of issue and expiry).
c You want to know about the same man's flight number, date and time of arrival.
d The office photocopier has broken down. You want to have it repaired quickly.

5.3 Apologising

> We must apologise for …
> We apologise for …
> We are extremely sorry for …
> Please accept our apologies for …

Note: Use the -*ing* form of a verb with these phrases, e.g. *We are extremely sorry for* **losing** *your order*.

Writing tip It is usually polite to apologise at the start, give the reason for the problem, and then apologise again at the end of the letter. (See Mona Stenlund's letter in 5.1.)

> Please accept our apologies once again.
> We hope that this has not caused you any inconvenience.
> With apologies once again, …

You received this email. How can you reply? (Apologise and give a reason.)

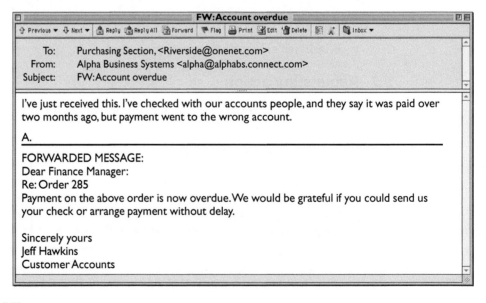

5.4 An unexpected reply

Sr Muñoz wanted more information from Haga Verktyg, so he sent another fax. Read his message and the reply, and answer the questions on page 52.

Fax +34 58 345545 19-05-2006 11:22 p.01

FAX COVER SHEET

CONSTRUCCIONES JIMÉNEZ

Avda del Pueblo Granada España
Tel/Fax +34 58 345545
info@jimenezcons.es
www.jimenezcons.es

For the attention of:	Export Manager
Organisation:	Haga Verktyg, Göteborg, Sweden
Fax No.	+46 31 638420
Date:	19 May 2006

Dear Ms Stenlund
Our order No. 2886

We have received your fax of 15 May, concerning the above order for five Kraftborr drills.

We were pleased to hear that you will ship the drills immediately. We would appreciate it, however, if you could give us further details about the delivery. In particular, we would like to know the name of the ship that you are using, the departure date from Sweden and the expected arrival date in Spain.

I look forward to hearing from you.
Yours

José Muñoz

Name: José Muñoz
Title/Department: Manager
No. of pages to follow: 0

18-06-2006   12:06 AVS.   HAGA VERKTYG   SWEDEN   +46 31 638420 p01

Your ref:
Our ref:

HV
HAGA VERKTYG

Kaponjärgatan 4c
Göteborg 41877
Sweden

Tel: +46 31 453423
Fax: +46 31 638420
hv@hagaverktyg.net.se

José Muñoz,
Manager, Purchasing
Construcciones Jiménez
Avda del Pueblo
Granada
Spain
Attention: J. Muñoz, Construcciones Jiménez

18 June 2006

Dear Sr Muñoz

Thank you for your fax of 19 May.

I regret to tell you that Haga Verktyg is no longer operating. We are therefore unable to supply the drills. We have passed all business on to Nordic Engineering who will contact you shortly.

With apologies

Mona Stenlund

Mona Stenlund

Haga Verktyg

a   What exactly did Sr Muñoz want to know? Why did he ask?
b   Sr Muñoz received an unexpected reply. Why can't Haga Verktyg supply the drills?
c   What do you think Sr Muñoz should do now?

5.5 Faxes

Messages sent by fax are similar to normal business letters. Some companies use their headed paper and write a normal letter which they then send by fax, whilst other companies use fax 'cover sheets', which show all the necessary information. The message is normally typed, but when the message is very short (such as a hotel booking confirmation), fax messages are sometimes handwritten in less formal English.

1   Look at the fax cover page from Construcciones Jiménez on page 48 and find this information. What does each one refer to?

a   0
b   16:04
c   +46 31 638420
d   José Muñoz
e   Manager, Purchasing
f   Export Manager
g   01
h   Haga Verktyg

2   **You work in the general office of a shipping company which transports goods all over the world. On page 53 is a blank fax cover sheet which you use in your office. What information would you write in the numbered spaces for each of these situations?**

a   You received an email yesterday from Ms D. Gentsler, EuroCargo, Händelstrasse 26, 6477 Limeshain, Germany (fax +49 6047 4894) asking for a list of your agents in Europe. The list is four pages long.

b   Your company wants to buy a Pantronic XP567 printer. You want to know what price RS Computer Supplies would charge for this (their total price including tax and delivery) and when they could deliver it. Their address is: 9 Charles Street, Perth, WA. Fax +9 474 1278.

c   You received a fax this morning from Toivonen Shipping. Unfortunately, the message was not clear and you could not read it. You want them to send it again. Their address is Laivanvarustajantatu 26, 00140 Helsinki, Finland. Fax +358 0 56 56 34.

d   You sent an email to Ms Zainab Badawi at ClearPrint Ltd this morning concerning a new design for your headed paper. You now want to fax three pages of design ideas to her. The address is 117 Chong Yip Street, Kwun Tong, Kowloon, Hong Kong. Fax +852 2878 7786.

Transglobe *Express*

239 Kanda Surugadai 2–chome
Chiyoda–ku
Tokyo 102-0065
Phone (81) 3 4578 6895
Fax (81) 3 4578 6866
transglobe@transglobesexpress.com.jp

FAX COVER SHEET

For the attention of: ❶   Date: ❷
Organisation: ❸   Fax No. ❹

Message: ❺

Name: ❻
Title/Department: ❼   No. of pages to follow: ❽

5.6 Consolidation: a complete fax cover letter

Your company, EverLite Ltd, a large electrical supplier, recently advertised for
a new store manager. Unfortunately, you have lost the application from
someone called Bernard Langé. You can find the letter he wrote with the
application, but not the application itself or the CV and photo he sent with it.
You now need to ask Mr Langé to send his complete application to you again.
Interviews are next week, so, to save time, you can fax the application forms
(five pages) to him and ask him to fax everything back to you. Write a fax
cover letter to Mr Langé explaining the situation. First, make a plan. Then
compare it with the one on page 123 before you write.

> What have you learned?
> Look back at the letter you wrote from Sunshine Airways at the beginning of this
> section. Compare it with your letter from EverLite Ltd in 5.6. Can you see an
> improvement?
> Think about:
> ● letter layout
> ● fax information
> ● ways to apologise
> ● ways to request action.

5B Activity section   From quote to sale

1   Tavridis are electrical contractors in Athens, Greece. They are working on some new houses and they now need 20,000 metres of 15-amp cable. To get a quotation, they sent the following email to a manufacturer.

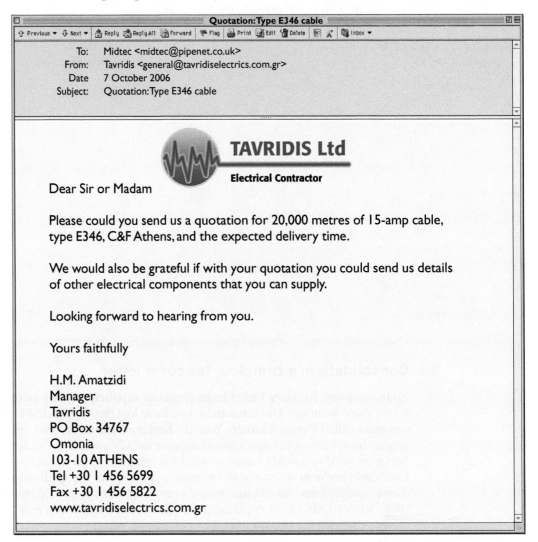

Quotation: Type E346 cable

Previous ▼   Next ▼   Reply   Reply All   Forward   Flag   Print   Edit   Delete   Inbox ▼

To: Midtec <midtec@pipenet.co.uk>
From: Tavridis <general@tavridiselectrics.com.gr>
Date   7 October 2006
Subject: Quotation: Type E346 cable

TAVRIDIS Ltd
Electrical Contractor

Dear Sir or Madam

Please could you send us a quotation for 20,000 metres of 15-amp cable, type E346, C&F Athens, and the expected delivery time.

We would also be grateful if with your quotation you could send us details of other electrical components that you can supply.

Looking forward to hearing from you.

Yours faithfully

H.M. Amatzidi
Manager
Tavridis
PO Box 34767
Omonia
103-10 ATHENS
Tel +30 1 456 5699
Fax +30 1 456 5822
www.tavridiselectrics.com.gr

2   A few days later, the building manager said that they needed the cable urgently. Mr Amatzidi therefore sent a message to another manufacturer for the same type of cable. He decided to send a fax, as he hoped it would receive immediate attention. Read his fax on page 55 and answer these questions.

a   Is Mr Amatzidi asking for the quote as soon as possible, or the cable as soon as possible?

b   How could he have written the message more clearly?

FAX MESSAGE

TAVRIDIS Ltd

Electrical Contractor

PO Box 34767, Omonia
103-10 ATHENS
Tel. +30 1 456 5699
Fax. +30 1 456 5822

For attention of: Sales Department
Organisation: Hanston Electrics Ltd
48 Golden Road, Manchester
M11 4NS England
Fax: +44 161 565342

Date: 10 October 2006

No. of pages: 1

MESSAGE:

Dear Sir or Madam

Please could you send us a quote for 20,000 metres of 15-amp cable, type E346, C&F Athens, with delivery time as soon as possible.

Yours faithfully

H. M. Amatzidi

Name: H.M. Amatzidi
Title/Department: Manager

3 Tavridis are now waiting for replies from the two manufacturers.
   In three groups, write the correspondence between them. When you have
   written an email, fax or letter, 'send' it to the correct group. Then ask for a
   new card number. (There are three cards for each company.)

Group 1

TAVRIDIS Ltd
Electrical Contractor
general@tavridiselectrics.com.gr
Fax: +30 1 456 5822
Start on card 19

Group 2

MIDTEC
CABLES LTD
midtec@pipenet.co.uk
Fax: +44 1392 929610
Start on card 7

Group 3

HANSTON
Electrics
sales@hanstonelectrics.com
Fax: +44 161 565342
Start on card 63

5C The writing process   Drafting

Very few people can write a message without first making draft versions, which they correct and revise. In this section, you can try two ways of writing a draft: *accurate writing* and *free writing*.

1 Accurate writing

In 'accurate writing', you only write what you know is correct, or you correct things immediately. You have ten minutes. You need to write the following email.

> You work in a watch-repair centre. People return watches to you for repair under guarantee. A woman has returned a watch to you, but it is not manufactured any more. Under the terms of the guarantee, she is entitled to a replacement. You have a similar one available. Does she want that one instead? Describe it (invent the details).

Make some notes, and write the main paragraph. Try *not* to make any mistakes. Only write what you think is correct. When you have finished, put your paper to one side and do Exercise 2.

> Dear Mrs Brown
> Thank you for returning your watch to us.

2 Free writing

In 'free writing', you write what comes into your head, without thinking about grammar, spelling, etc. Afterwards, you check and change what you have written. You have seven minutes. You need to write the following message.

> You have received a watch from a man. It arrived with the back of the watch open. You can see that he tried to repair it himself. Your guarantee does not cover that situation.

Make some quick notes and then write as much as you can. Don't worry about mistakes. *Just write!* After seven minutes, stop. You have three more minutes to check and change what you have done.

> Dear Mr Grey
> Thank you for returning your watch to us.

Compare what you wrote in Exercises 1 and 2. Which worked best for you? Compare with other students in the class.

Unit 6 Maintaining contact

6A Study section

- personal business letters and emails
- opening/closing
- inviting, accepting and declining

> **Test yourself**
>
> Last month, you met Lars Stenbok, from Sweden. He told you about his company's telecommunications products. You also met his colleague, Xu Cheng, who had a broken arm. You now want to invite Mr Stenbok to a dinner and presentation of your products. Write a full letter/email inviting him. (Invent any details that you need.)
>
> When you have finished, put the message away until the end of this section.

6.1 Michael Kennedy sends out some brochures

Michael Kennedy from EuroCom went to dinner with Khalid Al Jalahma from Arabian Electronics in Bahrain. Later, he sent Mr Al Jalahma details of a new product. He also sent the details to Ms Bugarini, who had written to him.

Look at messages a and b. Put ✔ (yes) or ✘ (no) for each point.
Is a or b more friendly? Why?

	a	b
The message opens with the main subject.		
The message mentions the last time they met.		
The message mentions personal information.		

a

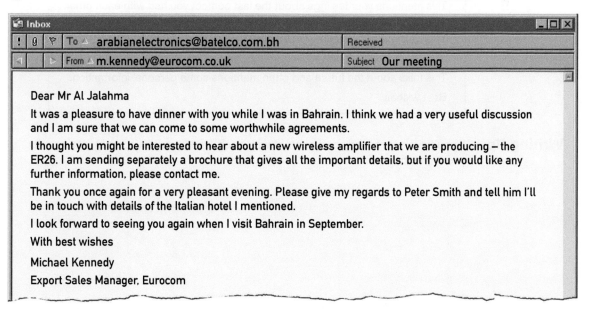

Inbox

To ▲ arabianelectronics@batelco.com.bh   Received

From ▲ m.kennedy@eurocom.co.uk   Subject **Our meeting**

Dear Mr Al Jalahma

It was a pleasure to have dinner with you while I was in Bahrain. I think we had a very useful discussion and I am sure that we can come to some worthwhile agreements.

I thought you might be interested to hear about a new wireless amplifier that we are producing – the ER26. I am sending separately a brochure that gives all the important details, but if you would like any further information, please contact me.

Thank you once again for a very pleasant evening. Please give my regards to Peter Smith and tell him I'll be in touch with details of the Italian hotel I mentioned.

I look forward to seeing you again when I visit Bahrain in September.

With best wishes

Michael Kennedy

Export Sales Manager, Eurocom

European Communications Company

16 Bedford Way   London W4 1HV
Tel: 020 1783 9576   Fax: 020 1763 7876
www.eurocom.co.uk

Ms R. Bugarini
Via Borsi 26
36543 Milan
Italy

5 July 2006

Dear Ms Bugarini

Thank you for your fax of 26 June, asking for details of our new wireless ER26 amplifier.

I have pleasure in enclosing our brochure. This gives details and prices of all our amplifiers.

If you require any further information, you can contact me directly on 020 1783 9565.

Yours sincerely

M S Kennedy

Michael Kennedy

Export Sales Manager

email: m.kennedy@eurocom.co.uk

6.2 Making a letter or email more personal

If you know the person that you are writing to and have met him/her socially, you will probably want to be less formal and more friendly. Less formal letters or emails often have a different structure from formal business letters or emails.

> Dear Mr/Ms/Mrs/Miss …
>
> *An opening*
> This mentions your feelings about the last contact you had with each other.
>
> *The main message*
> This says why you are writing now and gives the details.
>
> *The close*
> This talks about the future and often mentions some personal information.
>
> Best wishes

Writing tip   If you have not recently had contact with each other, you can open by saying why you are writing.

6.3 Personal business letters and emails: the opening

Here are some ways to open a less formal letter/email. You can talk about the last time you contacted – or could not contact – each other.

> Thank you for your letter/telephone call/email/fax.
> It was a pleasure to see you again at/on …
> It was good to hear from you again.
> It was a pity that we did not have more time to talk at/on …
> I am sorry that I missed you when you visited my office.

After each phrase you can add a comment.

> Thank you for your letter. *It was very interesting to hear about the new developments at Wentol.*
> It was good to talk to you on the telephone today. *I was sorry to hear that you had not been well.*
> Thank you for your fax. *I was pleased to hear that you will visit us next month.*

1 What opening would you write in each of these situations?

a You met the addressee on Thursday. She told you that she had been ill.
b You had dinner with the addressee last week at his house. He told you about his holiday in Iceland.
c You met the addressee in her office last week. She could only talk for five minutes.

If you are writing to someone you know and you want to be friendly, you can introduce the topic in a different way. Here are some examples.

Requesting action	I was wondering if you could help me.
Giving information	I thought you might be interested to hear about …
Complaining	I am afraid we have a small problem.
Giving bad news	I am afraid I have some bad news.

2 Fill in the gaps in the letter and email.

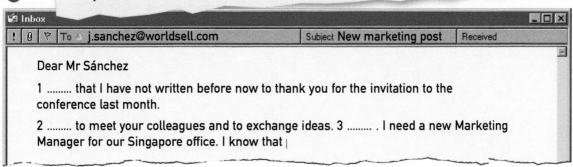

a

Dear Mrs Poirot
1 ……… the invitation to the exhibition last week. 2 ……… to see the range of products that you produce. 3 ……… a new service that we have just introduced. This is the Golden Maintenance Agreement. For a fixed price, we can offer 24-hour emergency repairs for …

b

Inbox

To j.sanchez@worldsell.com   Subject **New marketing post**   Received

Dear Mr Sánchez

1 ……… that I have not written before now to thank you for the invitation to the conference last month.

2 ……… to meet your colleagues and to exchange ideas. 3 ……… . I need a new Marketing Manager for our Singapore office. I know that

6.4 Personal business letters and emails: the close

Less formal letters and emails often close by mentioning something personal.

> I look forward to seeing you again next time I am in Taipei.
> If you are ever in London, please give me a ring or stop by my office.

Sometimes, you can mention somebody that you both know.

> Please give my regards to Diana Smith.
> Please pass on my best wishes to Mr Lund. I hope that he has now recovered
>   from the flu.

6.5 Practice

This message is mixed up. Put the sentences in the correct order and divide the message into paragraphs.

Dear Ms Weinburger

a   Please give my regards to Steven Hill.

b   It was interesting to hear your views on our new products.

c   I would be very grateful, therefore, if you could recommend any agents to me. We have found lots on the Internet, but it is difficult to know which ones are reliable or well established.

d   As you know, our company is planning to open a branch in Los Angeles.

e   I was wondering if you could help me.

f   It was a pleasure to meet you at the Trade Fair last month.

g   We are now looking for office space in the town centre and we need to know the names and addresses of some property agents.

Yours sincerely

Hans Seitz

Hans Seitz
Divisional Director

6.6 Michael Kennedy receives some invitations

A few days after he wrote to Arabian Electronics, Michael Kennedy received this reply. He also received an invitation from SpyFi Communications, so he checked his digital diary. What replies should he give to each invitation? Who should he write to?

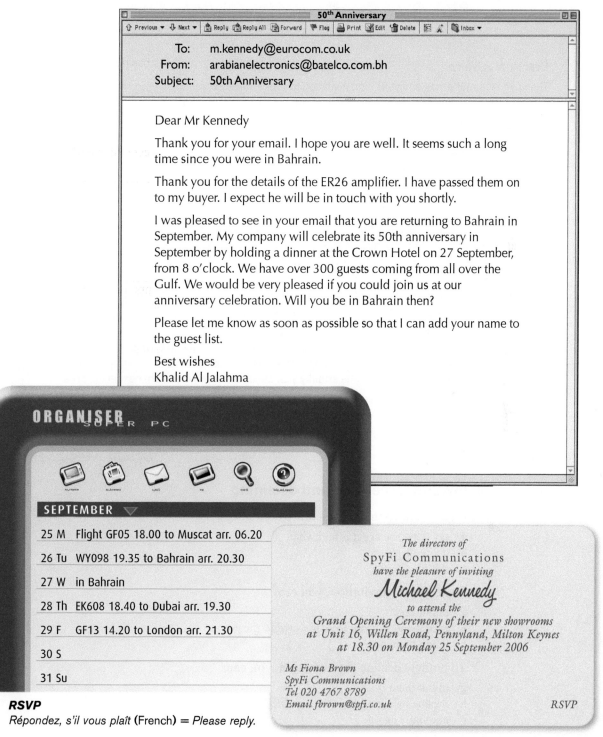

50th Anniversary

⇧ Previous ▼ ⇩ Next ▼ 📋 Reply 📋 Reply All 📋 Forward 🚩 Flag 🖨 Print 📝 Edit 🗑 Delete 📧 A⁺ 📁 Inbox ▼

To: m.kennedy@eurocom.co.uk
From: arabianelectronics@batelco.com.bh
Subject: 50th Anniversary

Dear Mr Kennedy

Thank you for your email. I hope you are well. It seems such a long time since you were in Bahrain.

Thank you for the details of the ER26 amplifier. I have passed them on to my buyer. I expect he will be in touch with you shortly.

I was pleased to see in your email that you are returning to Bahrain in September. My company will celebrate its 50th anniversary in September by holding a dinner at the Crown Hotel on 27 September, from 8 o'clock. We have over 300 guests coming from all over the Gulf. We would be very pleased if you could join us at our anniversary celebration. Will you be in Bahrain then?

Please let me know as soon as possible so that I can add your name to the guest list.

Best wishes
Khalid Al Jalahma

ORGANISER SUPER PC

SEPTEMBER

25 M	Flight GF05 18.00 to Muscat arr. 06.20
26 Tu	WY098 19.35 to Bahrain arr. 20.30
27 W	in Bahrain
28 Th	EK608 18.40 to Dubai arr. 19.30
29 F	GF13 14.20 to London arr. 21.30
30 S	
31 Su	

The directors of
SpyFi Communications
have the pleasure of inviting

Michael Kennedy

to attend the
Grand Opening Ceremony of their new showrooms
at Unit 16, Willen Road, Pennyland, Milton Keynes
at 18.30 on Monday 25 September 2006

Ms Fiona Brown
SpyFi Communications
Tel 020 4767 8789
Email fbrown@spfi.co.uk   RSVP

RSVP
Répondez, s'il vous plaît (French) = *Please reply.*

6.7 Michael Kennedy replies

Michael Kennedy replied to each invitation. What did he say to accept or decline each invitation? What did he say about the future in each reply?

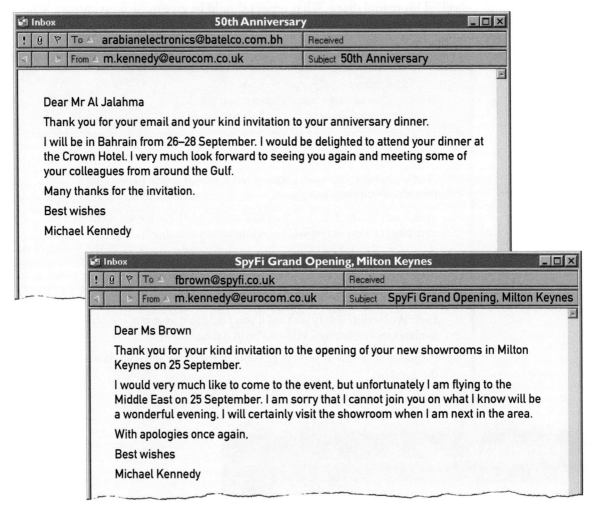

Inbox — 50th Anniversary

To △ arabianelectronics@batelco.com.bh Received
From △ m.kennedy@eurocom.co.uk Subject 50th Anniversary

Dear Mr Al Jalahma

Thank you for your email and your kind invitation to your anniversary dinner.

I will be in Bahrain from 26–28 September. I would be delighted to attend your dinner at the Crown Hotel. I very much look forward to seeing you again and meeting some of your colleagues from around the Gulf.

Many thanks for the invitation.

Best wishes

Michael Kennedy

Inbox — SpyFi Grand Opening, Milton Keynes

To △ fbrown@spyfi.co.uk Received
From △ m.kennedy@eurocom.co.uk Subject SpyFi Grand Opening, Milton Keynes

Dear Ms Brown

Thank you for your kind invitation to the opening of your new showrooms in Milton Keynes on 25 September.

I would very much like to come to the event, but unfortunately I am flying to the Middle East on 25 September. I am sorry that I cannot join you on what I know will be a wonderful evening. I will certainly visit the showroom when I am next in the area.

With apologies once again,

Best wishes

Michael Kennedy

6.8 Inviting, accepting and declining

If you want to invite someone by letter, email or fax, you can:

a say what the event is and when
b invite them
c ask for a reply.

To accept the invitation, you can:

d thank them
e accept and say you look forward to the event
f thank them again.

To politely decline the invitation, you can:

g thank them
h decline by giving a reason; apologise and say you are disappointed
i apologise again.

1 Look back at the messages in 6.6 and 6.7 Write the correct letter (a–i) beside the relevant part of each message.

Here are some more phrases you can use.

Inviting	We would be very pleased if you could join us at …
	We would be delighted if you could come to …
	We have pleasure in inviting you to …
Accepting	I would be delighted to join you at …
	I would be very pleased to …
	I am very happy to accept your invitation to …
Declining	I would very much like to come, but unfortunately …
	Unfortunately, I will not be able to join you because …
	I am so sorry, but I cannot come to … because …

2 Your company will soon launch a new range of baby products called BabyTime. Write an invitation to a special pre-launch buffet reception.

3 Write a message accepting and a message declining this invitation.

Dear …
Next month, on the 23rd, we are holding our Summer Party. This is an annual event, which is always a great occasion. The main feature of the party is the Grand Karaoke Competition. It's great fun.
We're forming teams, so were wondering if you and your colleagues would like to come. We hope that you're free on 23 August and that you can join us.
Best wishes
Sarah Williams
Marketing Manager

6.9 Consolidation: a complete letter or email

You work in the computer section of StorFinans Bank, Sweden. Recently, you met Anneka van Ek on a training course. She gave a talk about computer security. She invited you to a workshop next week, but you can't go because you have a meeting. However, you want to invite her to a conference on Information Technology at your bank next month to give the same talk on computer security. Write to her at avanek@compusoft.org. Make a plan and compare it with the one on page 123 before you write the message.

> **What have you learned?**
> Look back at the message you wrote to Lars Stenbok at the beginning of this section. Compare it with your message to Anneka van Ek in 6.9. Can you see an improvement? Think about:
> - layout
> - being friendly in personal messages
> - inviting and accepting/declining.

6B Activity section　　Repair or replace?

1 Jarritos is a small company in Spain that makes bottled soft drinks. The General Manager, Raul Sánchez, wants to modernise their equipment. He saw this advertisement on the Internet. Read it and answer these questions.

a Does the Alpha Rapid Bottler use disposable bottles?

b Can it bottle fizzy soft drinks?

Alpha Food Systems – The Rapid Bottler – ▢✕

Introducing ... *The Alpha Rapid Bottler*

NEW from Alpha!

The Alpha Rapid Bottler is completely computer controlled, offering you trouble-free bottling. It can handle up to 100* reusable bottles a minute and

- washes the bottles in boiling water
- checks for cracked and broken bottles
- fills each bottle to the required level and caps them
- puts labels on the bottles
- packs the bottles into crates
- can run 24 hours a day with minimum maintenance.

* Still liquids; gassed liquids 50% of speed.

Contact **Alpha Food Machines, 54 Rue Barrault, Toulouse 31000, France. Tel/Fax +33 56 81 38 58 29**
or write to our <u>Sales Consultants</u> at <u>sales@alpha.fr</u> to arrange a visit to your company.

Mr Sánchez decided to ask Alpha to visit his company. He sent this email to the Sales Consultants.

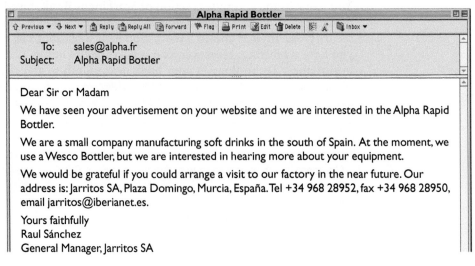

To: sales@alpha.fr
Subject: Alpha Rapid Bottler

Dear Sir or Madam

We have seen your advertisement on your website and we are interested in the Alpha Rapid Bottler.

We are a small company manufacturing soft drinks in the south of Spain. At the moment, we use a Wesco Bottler, but we are interested in hearing more about your equipment.

We would be grateful if you could arrange a visit to our factory in the near future. Our address is: Jarritos SA, Plaza Domingo, Murcia, España. Tel +34 968 28952, fax +34 968 28950, email jarritos@iberianet.es.

Yours faithfully
Raul Sánchez
General Manager, Jarritos SA

2 Shortly after Mr Sánchez wrote to Alpha, Jarritos' own bottling machine started causing some problems. He therefore wrote to Wesco. Read the email he wrote and answer the following question.

What is the main difference between the Wesco bottler and the Alpha Rapid bottler?

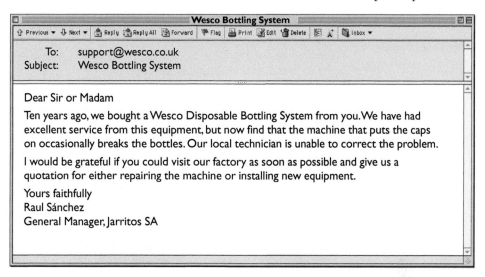

To: support@wesco.co.uk
Subject: Wesco Bottling System

Dear Sir or Madam

Ten years ago, we bought a Wesco Disposable Bottling System from you. We have had excellent service from this equipment, but now find that the machine that puts the caps on occasionally breaks the bottles. Our local technician is unable to correct the problem.

I would be grateful if you could visit our factory as soon as possible and give us a quotation for either repairing the machine or installing new equipment.

Yours faithfully
Raul Sánchez
General Manager, Jarritos SA

3 Within the next few days, consultants from both Wesco (Mr Tony Smith) and Alpha (Ms Françoise Molet) made separate visits to Jarritos. Mr Sánchez showed them round the factory and introduced them to Cristina Barrios, Technical Manager. Later, they had dinner at Mr Sánchez's home. The consultants told him they would send him quotations soon. Jarritos is now waiting to hear from Wesco and Alpha. In three groups, you must write the correspondence between the three companies. When you have written a letter, email or fax, 'send' it to the correct group. Then ask for a new card number. (There are three cards for each group.)

Group 1	Group 2	Group 3

jarritos@iberianet.es

Start on card 37

sales@alpha.fr

Start on card 49

support@wesco.co.uk

Start on card 21

6C The writing process — Checking your work (1)

Before you send a message, it is always useful to check it! You can ask yourself three questions.

- Is the English accurate?
- Is the style and level of formality appropriate?
- Is it clear?

The first question is addressed in this section. The second and third questions are addressed in Sections 7C and 8C.

1 Is the English accurate?

There are three main areas you can check.

Punctuation **Spelling** **Grammar**

Work with a partner. What things can you check under each area? Make a list. When you are ready, compare with other students in the class and the list on page 123.

2 Your frequent mistakes

What are your most frequent mistakes? Look carefully at your past work in English and make a list of the mistakes you make. You can try to make a mnemonic – a word that will help you remember what to check. For example:

> S I P P A
> 'S' at the end of verbs ('She works')
> –Ing after some verbs ('stop making')
> Past simple ('did') and present perfect
> ('have done')
> Prepositions ('on', 'at', 'in', 'by')
> Adjectives before nouns

You can use your mnemonic to check everything you write in English.

Unit 7 Customer service

7A Study section

- informal business letters
- informal writing style
- replying to complaints
- advising customers

> **Test yourself**
>
> Four years ago, you worked with Adriana Lima. Last week, you met her again. She has started a new job as the CEO of a large software company. Your company, an electrical contractor, recently installed the lights in her office. She told you that the lights keep overheating and burning out. You have investigated this and have discovered that there is a fault with the ventilation on those types of light. You will send a technician to correct the problem next week. Write to Adriana Lima and tell her this. (Invent any details that you need.)
>
> When you have finished, put the message away until the end of this section.

7.1 Michael Kennedy writes to some business friends

Michael Kennedy is now friends with many of the people he meets on his business trips. Here are some emails and a fax he wrote to them about his company's new amplifier.

1 Which letter or message is:
a giving advice?
b accepting a complaint?
c rejecting a complaint?

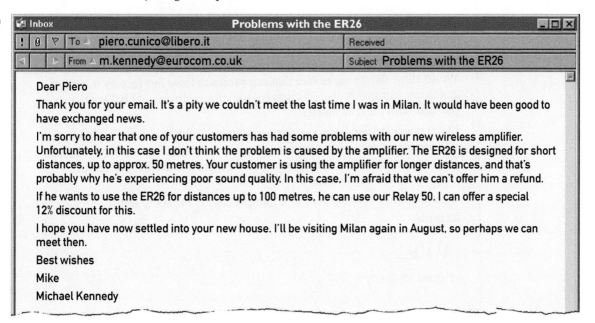

Inbox — **Problems with the ER26**

To: piero.cunico@libero.it   Received:

From: m.kennedy@eurocom.co.uk   Subject: **Problems with the ER26**

Dear Piero

Thank you for your email. It's a pity we couldn't meet the last time I was in Milan. It would have been good to have exchanged news.

I'm sorry to hear that one of your customers has had some problems with our new wireless amplifier. Unfortunately, in this case I don't think the problem is caused by the amplifier. The ER26 is designed for short distances, up to approx. 50 metres. Your customer is using the amplifier for longer distances, and that's probably why he's experiencing poor sound quality. In this case, I'm afraid that we can't offer him a refund.

If he wants to use the ER26 for distances up to 100 metres, he can use our Relay 50. I can offer a special 12% discount for this.

I hope you have now settled into your new house. I'll be visiting Milan again in August, so perhaps we can meet then.

Best wishes

Mike

Michael Kennedy

②

!	⊌	℗	To △ j.thijseen@hollandnet.nl	Received
◁		▷	From △ m.kennedy@eurocom.co.uk	Subject ER26 and music

Dear Jan

Thanks for your email. It was good to hear from you again.

You asked if it was possible to use our new wireless amplifier for live music. I'm sorry to say that I wouldn't recommend it. The ER26 is mainly intended for speech. If you are looking for an amplifier similar to the ER26 but with a wider frequency range, I suggest you contact Melitronics (melitronics@compunet.co.uk) in Birmingham. They make several good-quality amplifiers, similar to the ER26. Unfortunately they are all more expensive.

Alternatively, you might prefer to use our TD354 amplifier and connect it to our Jump 2 wireless broadcast system. I have attached some more details for you.

If you are ever in London, please don't forget to give me a call. Perhaps we can meet for lunch.

Regards

Mike

Michael Kennedy

③

15-07-2006 15:37 Eurocom → Abdullah Al Harrasi + 44 20 1763 7876

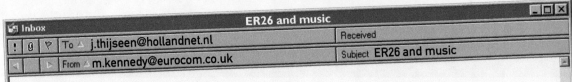

EuroCom
European Communications Company

16 Bedford Way   London W4 1HV
Tel: 020 1783 9576   Fax: 020 1763 7876
www.eurocom.co.uk

FAX

Abdullah Al Harrasi
Fax: 00 968 793 286
Total: 1 page

15 July 2006

Dear Abdullah

Thank you for your fax.

I was sorry to hear that one of your customers has had problems with the ER26. We do all we can to make sure that our products leave our factory in perfect condition, but unfortunately mistakes sometimes do occur. I believe there's a problem with the transmitter.

I've arranged to send you a replacement immediately. I've also included a free B3 wireless microphone to compensate your customer for the inconvenience. The courier will collect the defective model from you so that you're not inconvenienced any further.

With apologies once again, and hoping that you're keeping well.

Regards

Mike

Michael Kennedy

2 Look at the three messages on pages 67 and 68 again. Put ✔ or ✘ for each point.

	message 1	message 2	message 3
contractions (e.g. *I'm*)			
first names to open and close			
full name and title of the writer			

7.2 Informal business letters and emails

If you are a friend of the person that you are writing to, you will want to make your letter informal, as Michael Kennedy has done. Notice how he:

- opens with the addressee's first name
- uses contractions
- uses short, direct phrases
- uses a friendly style and makes personal comments
- signs with his first name (i.e. not his title).

Writing tip The use of first names varies from culture to culture. In Europe and in English-speaking cultures, first names are frequently used in business correspondence. In other cultures, this may cause offence. If you are in doubt, use the same style that the addressee uses to you.

7.3 Informal language: short phrases and contractions

Informal written language is much closer to spoken English than the language used in formal letters. For example, in spoken English we often use contractions, like this:

> I'm going for a walk.   I'd like a cup of coffee.

In the same way, contractions are often used in informal written language.

> It's a pity that we couldn't meet.   I'm enclosing some brochures.

1 Look at Michael Kennedy's messages in 7.1. What contractions does he use?

Here is a very simple rule that is usually (but not always!) true:

Longer phrases are more formal than shorter phrases.

For example:

> I would be grateful if you could tell me your prices.

is more formal than:

> Please could you possibly tell me your prices?

and that is more formal than:

> Please can you tell me your prices?

2 Look at the following twelve sentences and group together those which have a similar meaning. You should have four groups. Then put the sentences in each group in order according to how formal they are, with the most formal first.

a If you need any more information, please feel free to ask me.
b I am in receipt of your letter dated 16 March.
c When do you think the goods will get here?
d I am writing in connection with your advertisement in *The News*.
e I have just seen your advert in *The News*.
f Thanks for your letter of 16 March.
g Please could you tell me when the goods will arrive?
h If you'd like any more details, please ask me.
i I would appreciate it if you could tell me when the goods will arrive.
j Thank you for your letter dated 16 March.
k If you require any further information, please do not hesitate to contact me.
l I am writing with reference to your advertisement in *The News*.

7.4 Informal language: vocabulary

Some words sound more formal than other words. For example:

> I regret to advise you that our prices have increased.

sounds more formal than:

> I am sorry to say that our prices have gone up.

In the same way:

> We have not yet received your invoice.

sounds more formal than:

> We have not yet got your bill.

1 Read these sentences, and match the words in *italics* with the words in the box below.

a I am writing to *enquire* about your prices.
b This is *due to the fact that* our costs have risen.
c If you *require* any *further* information, please contact me.
d I *regret* to *advise* you that the delivery will be delayed.
e Unfortunately, I have to *inform* you that I *will not be able to attend* the meeting.
f *Please find enclosed* some brochures describing our products.
g We have *been forced to* increase our prices.
h We have opened a letter of credit *in your favour*.

> cannot come to   more   here are   tell   for you
> because   tell   need   am sorry   ask   had to

2 **Now rewrite these sentences so that they sound less formal.**

a I have pleasure in enclosing a cheque in your favour.

b I am pleased to inform you that your application for a post as secretary was successful.

c I regret to advise you that we will not be able to deliver the goods on time.

d I would be grateful if you could advise me of your prices.

e Please find enclosed our invoice.

7.5 Practice

Here is a formal business letter. Rewrite it so that it sounds more friendly and informal. Remember to look back at 7.2 and 7.3 and Unit 6A.

Cornfields Pesticides Co Ltd
39 THE HILL, BURTON, SUSSEX BN5 9TJ   Tel 01273 52663

Mr Richard Scott
Welsh Garden Suppliers
Cardiff
CF4 2FT

Your ref.
Our ref. GW/pk
22 Jan 2006

Dear Mr Scott

I am writing in connection with your telephone order of 16 January, in which you enquired about our KILL'EM fly spray.

Unfortunately, I regret to inform you that we stopped producing and distributing this fly spray last year due to the fact that we now specialise in agricultural products. I suggest you contact Brown's Online Home Supplies, www.brownonline.co.uk., as they purchased all our stock.

With apologies once again.

Yours sincerely

S Wollen.

Sarah Wollen
Sales Executive

email cornfield@uknet.co.uk

7.6 Replying to complaints

If you want to accept a complaint, you can:

- apologise for the problem
- explain what caused it
- say what action you will take
- apologise again.

If you want to reject a complaint, you can:

- say you are sorry they had problems
- explain why you think it is not your fault
- say what you can do (optional)
- offer a solution (optional).

1 **Look back at 7.1. Can you find the same structure in Michael Kennedy's letters?**

2 **Read these two complaints. Are they formal or informal? Do you think you should accept them or reject them? What would you write?**

a

Dear Jack

How are you? I'm busy as usual. I've just got back from London.

I was wondering if you could help me. I bought one of your TX308 phones and I have a problem with the power unit. The phone works well, but when I plugged the charger in last night, there was a strong burning smell, and smoke started to come from inside the charger. I enclose the charger so you can see.

Some of my colleagues told me that they think they saw a notice in the newspaper last week, asking customers to return their TX308 chargers because of a fault. Is that right? Could you get it checked for me and see if you can get it replaced? Many thanks!

Hope you're ready for the holidays. I really need one!

Thanks again

b

Dear Sir or Madam

I am writing about the poor quality of your mobile telephones.

Last week, I purchased a model TX308. Among the many features of the telephone, the sales assistant said that the body of the phone would survive a fall to the ground. Yesterday, however, I placed the telephone on the roof of my car. I drove away and then, in my mirror, I saw the telephone fly off the roof and fall to the ground. I stopped to pick it up, but found it in pieces. The screen is smashed, the body is smashed, and the battery has broken in half. I enclose the telephone.

I would therefore like to request that you refund my money for this telephone, or give me a suitable replacement.

Yours faithfully

7.7 Advising customers

Sometimes, you may need to give customers advice. You can:

- say you are sorry you cannot help them directly
- say why
- suggest what they can do instead.

Look at Michael Kennedy's second email in 7.1.

To suggest, you can say:

I recommend that you …	contact …
You could …	try …
You might prefer to …	use …
I suggest you …	email …

What would you write to these people?

a Your company stopped making Sun Yellow paint last year. A man telephoned you today because he wants a small quantity of paint to repaint a wall. You have now found out that he can make the same colour by mixing your Corn Yellow with your Lemon Yellow.

b Ben emailed you to ask for your help. You have known Ben for three years (he is married to a friend of yours). He has knocked over a tin of your paint on his wooden floor and he cannot get the paint off. Your paint is a permanent paint. The only answer is to replace the wood.

c A woman applied by letter for a job in your office. There are no vacancies now, but you may have some jobs available next January.

7.8 Consolidation: a complete letter or email

Last week, you met Silvio Puchetti, a business friend whom you had not seen for years. You talked for a long time about a new bakery that he has started, which is now very successful. Silvio told you that your company installed the ovens that he uses.

Unfortunately, he complained that the ovens very frequently burn the bottom of the bread. You have investigated this and have discovered that he is putting too many loaves into the oven at the same time. The only solution is to put fewer loaves in the oven or buy a larger oven. You can give him a discount for this.

Write to Silvio and tell him this. First, make a plan. Then compare it with the plan on page 123 before you write the message.

What have you learned?
Look back at the message you wrote to Adriana Lima at the beginning of this section. Compare it with your message to Silvio Puchetti in 7.8. Can you see an improvement? Think about:
- language in informal letters
- accepting/rejecting complaints
- advising.

7B Activity section   A credit check

1   Wainman (Printers) Ltd want to order some paper on credit. Harold
    Wainman, one of the owners, telephoned Paula Robinson at Northern
    Paperworks to ask if this was possible. She asked him to put the request in
    writing. This is the letter he faxed to her.

a Does Harold Wainman know Paula Robinson? How do you know?

b Why does Harold Wainman want the paper on credit?

WAINMAN 01539 486783 _ 01524 767545 12:03 13-11-06 page 1/1

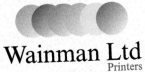

Wainman Ltd
Printers

Paula Robinson   Castle Street
Northern Paperworks   Kendal LA9 5YY
Old Mill   Tel/Fax 01539 486783
Horwich   wainman@networld.co.uk
Lancs BL6 5JA

                                                      13 November 2006

Dear Paula

This is to confirm the details of my telephone call this morning.

As I explained, we've received some very large orders for
printing which need to be done within the next two weeks.
As we won't receive payment for these orders until much later,
I asked if Northern Paperworks would be able to supply
us on credit. I've attached details of the materials that we
require to complete these orders.

If you need a credit reference for your files, you could write to
Pelican Paper Ltd, College Court, College Road, London, email
pelican@pelicanpaper.co.uk.

I hope that you're keeping well. Please say hello to David for
me. I look forward to hearing from you.

Best wishes

Harold

Harold Wainman.

Directors: H. Wainman and N. Lollerwicz

---

2   Northern Paperworks emailed Pelican Paper to ask for a reference.
    Their correspondence is shown on the next page. Do Pelican Paper think
    Wainman are reliable?

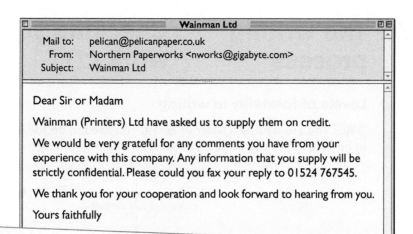

Wainman Ltd

Mail to: pelican@pelicanpaper.co.uk
From: Northern Paperworks <nworks@gigabyte.com>
Subject: Wainman Ltd

Dear Sir or Madam

Wainman (Printers) Ltd have asked us to supply them on credit.

We would be very grateful for any comments you have from your experience with this company. Any information that you supply will be strictly confidential. Please could you fax your reply to 01524 767545.

We thank you for your cooperation and look forward to hearing from you.

Yours faithfully

---

17 Nov 06 PELICAN +44 870 7675982 TO: 01524 767545 1/1 pages

Pelican Paper Ltd
College Court
College Road
London N21 3LL

Tel/Fax 0870 7675982
www.pelicanpaper.co.uk

PELICAN
PAPER Ltd

Northern Paperworks
Fax 01524 767545
17 November 2006

Dear Ms Robinson

Thank you for your email of 15 November, enquiring about Wainman Ltd.

We have been dealing with this company for over six years. During this time, they have always settled their accounts with us promptly, and we have never had any reason for complaint.

I hope that this information is of use to you.

Yours sincerely

N Lollerwicz

N. Lollerwicz

---

3 Wainman Ltd are now waiting for a reply from Northern Paperworks. Meanwhile, Northern Paperworks decided they wanted another credit reference, so they contacted Claire Brown at Lumino Inks. In three groups, you must write the correspondence between the three companies. Decide if you need a formal or informal style. When you have written a letter, email or fax, 'send' it to the correct group. Then ask for a new card number. (There are three cards for each group.)

Group 1	Group 2	Group 3

Wainman Ltd
Printers
wainman@networld.co.uk
Start on card 64

Northern Paperworks
nworks@gigabyte.com
Start on card 43

LUMINO INKS LTD
Claire@Luminoinks.co.uk
Start on card 34

7C The writing process   Checking your work (2)

1 Levels of formality in writing

When you are writing a letter or email, you need to decide how formal it needs to be. It is important to think about *who* you are writing to.

Do you know the person you are writing to?

No.   Yes, but not very well.   Yes, quite well. I can be quite relaxed with him/her.

A formal style is the safest.   Use a personal, semi-formal style.   Use an informal style.

2 What makes a message more or less formal?

In Units 6A and 7A, you saw some ways to make messages less formal. Can you put each of the following under the appropriate heading? Some items can go under two or more headings.

- Use formal, written language
- Use contractions
- Use exclamation marks
- Use first names
- Use job titles
- Use long sentences
- Use *Mr/Mrs/Ms* + surname
- Use shorter sentences
- Use spoken English forms
- Mention personal information/feelings
- Mention the last time you met
- Mention something personal to the addressee

a formal style	a personal, semi-formal style	an informal style

3 Some examples

Are these messages formal, semi-formal or informal? How do you know?

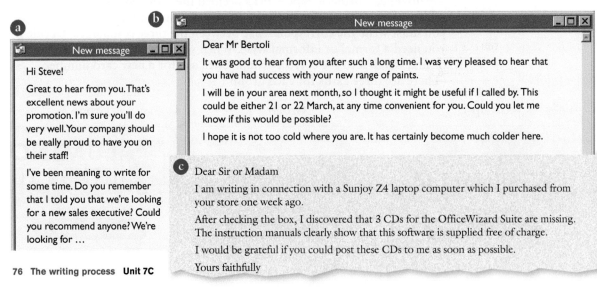

a

New message

Hi Steve!

Great to hear from you. That's excellent news about your promotion. I'm sure you'll do very well. Your company should be really proud to have you on their staff!

I've been meaning to write for some time. Do you remember that I told you that we're looking for a new sales executive? Could you recommend anyone? We're looking for …

b

New message

Dear Mr Bertoli

It was good to hear from you after such a long time. I was very pleased to hear that you have had success with your new range of paints.

I will be in your area next month, so I thought it might be useful if I called by. This could be either 21 or 22 March, at any time convenient for you. Could you let me know if this would be possible?

I hope it is not too cold where you are. It has certainly become much colder here.

c Dear Sir or Madam

I am writing in connection with a Sunjoy Z4 laptop computer which I purchased from your store one week ago.

After checking the box, I discovered that 3 CDs for the OfficeWizard Suite are missing. The instruction manuals clearly show that this software is supplied free of charge.

I would be grateful if you could post these CDs to me as soon as possible.

Yours faithfully

Unit 8 Product promotion

8A Study section

- arranging and confirming meetings
- placing orders
- circulars
- revision and consolidation

8.1 Introducing new products

Universal Books Ltd is a small publisher. They have just published two new books. Nigel Westwood is a sales executive and he has written letters to bookshop managers to introduce the books and to make an appointment to visit.

1 Put the paragraphs of his letter in the correct order.

2 If a shop had one copy of each of the new items (books and disks), how many items would it have?

Your ref

Our ref NW/lea

Universal Books Ltd

PO Box 379 Jersey, Channel Islands
Tel. 01534-797201
Fax 01534-797407
books@universal.net
www.universal.net

Ms M. Russell
Ashworth Bookshops Ltd
234 Hogden Road
Bristol BS7 9XS

23 July 2006

Dear Ms Russell

a   Both of these books are very competitively priced, and we offer attractive discounts to booksellers. I enclose sample sections from both titles for you to review.

b   After years of research, we have now produced THE WORLDWIDE ENCYCLOPAEDIA, an important new work for the home and schools, containing information on thousands of subjects. It is available as a set of three volumes, as a one-volume shorter edition and as a multimedia DVD, with built-in links to the Internet.

c   On 21–22 August, I will be in your area and I would be very grateful if I could meet you and show you our new books. Would Tuesday, 22 August at 11.30 a.m. be convenient for you?

d   I am writing to introduce two important new titles just published by Universal.

e   I will telephone you next week to confirm. I look forward to meeting you.

f   Our second new title is THE COMPLETE COLLECTION OF BUSINESS LETTERS, containing 3,000 ready-to-use letters. All a business person has to do is choose the letter that they want, make a few small changes and then print it off or click to send it by email. It is available in hardback and paperback, each with an accompanying CD-ROM.

Yours sincerely

N. Westwood

Nigel Westwood
Sales Executive

8.2 Arranging a meeting

Here is Margaret Russell's digital diary entry for 21 and 22 August.

1 Can she meet Nigel Westwood on the day and at the time he suggested?

2 Write her reply to Nigel Westwood. Suggest some other days and times for them to meet.

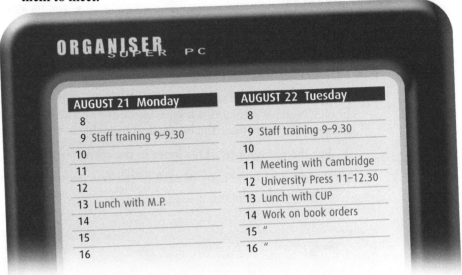

ORGANISER SUPER PC

AUGUST 21 Monday

8

9 Staff training 9–9.30

10

11

12

13 Lunch with M.P.

14

15

16

AUGUST 22 Tuesday

8

9 Staff training 9–9.30

10

11 Meeting with Cambridge

12 University Press 11–12.30

13 Lunch with CUP

14 Work on book orders

15 "

16 "

8.3 Confirming the details of a meeting

After their meeting, Nigel Westwood wrote to confirm the details of their discussion and to tell Ms Russell that he was waiting for her order. Here is part of his email.

1 Write the beginning and ending of Nigel Westwood's email. (Remember that he has met Margaret Russell, so his email will be more personal.)

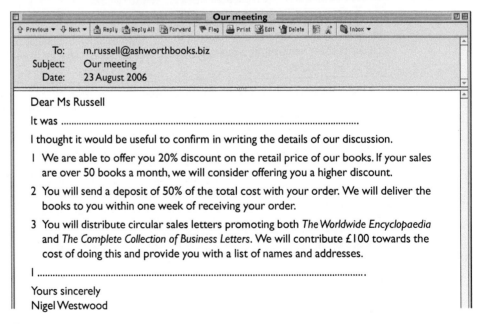

Our meeting

⇧ Previous ▾ ⬇ Next ▾ | 🖹 Reply 🖹 Reply All 🖹 Forward | 🏳 Flag | 🖨 Print 🖹 Edit 🗑 Delete | 📧 🗛 | 📥 Inbox ▾

To: m.russell@ashworthbooks.biz
Subject: Our meeting
Date: 23 August 2006

Dear Ms Russell

It was ....

I thought it would be useful to confirm in writing the details of our discussion.

1 We are able to offer you 20% discount on the retail price of our books. If your sales are over 50 books a month, we will consider offering you a higher discount.

2 You will send a deposit of 50% of the total cost with your order. We will deliver the books to you within one week of receiving your order.

3 You will distribute circular sales letters promoting both *The Worldwide Encyclopaedia* and *The Complete Collection of Business Letters*. We will contribute £100 towards the cost of doing this and provide you with a list of names and addresses.

I ....

Yours sincerely
Nigel Westwood

2 What does Margaret Russell have to send with her order?

3 How will Universal Books Ltd help Ashworth Bookshops to promote the books in their area?

8.4 Placing an order

Some days later, Margaret Russell made out her first order for the books.

20 sets of 3-volume 'Worldwide Encyclopaedia'
50 shorter 'Worldwide Encyclopaedia'
50 DVD edition

20 'Complete Business Letters' (hardback)
50 'Complete Business Letters' (paperback)

Write Ms Russell's letter to Nigel Westwood, placing the order. Remember that she must also send the deposit.

8.5 Writing a circular

Margaret Russell's next task was to write a circular sales letter to send to local schools. First, she made notes about the encyclopaedia from the information that Nigel Westwood had given her.

'Worldwide Encyclopaedia'

- Over half a million sold
- For parents, students and children
- Large detailed index and homework section
- Direct links from the school syllabus to the encyclopaedia
- Large, clear print
- Over 1,000 photos and other images

- Multimedia DVD has automatic updates from the Internet
- Search → half a second
- Intelligent Scanning chooses the most relevant material for each query
- Price £25 (shorter), £45 (3 vol.), £35 DVD
- Refund within 28 days

1 Read her letter and find answers to these questions.

a Is Margaret Russell's letter a formal business letter?
b Why did Margaret Russell write the letter like this?
c Did she use all her notes?

ASHWORTH
BOOKSHOPS LTD

234 Hogden Rd   Bristol BS7 9XS   Tel. 0800 9340

ANNOUNCING AN IMPORTANT NEW BOOK AND CD-ROM FOR THE HOME AND SCHOOL
THE WORLDWIDE ENCYCLOPAEDIA

Parents!

Do you and your children spend hours trying to find information for school? Are you fed up with sifting through mountains of irrelevant web pages?

Now, all your troubles are over! THE WORLDWIDE ENCYCLOPAEDIA has all the answers you'll ever need!

It's easy! Just look in the **large detailed index** for the information that you want or consult the **Homework Resource Section** and the **direct links** to the school syllabuses. THE WORLDWIDE ENCYCLOPAEDIA contains thousands of entries. It's quick and easy to use and will save you hours. It has over **1,000 full-colour photographs** and **maps, charts and useful tables** – all the things that your child needs for school.

THE WORLDWIDE ENCYCLOPAEDIA is a must for every family. There are two paper editions – a full **three-volume set** (£45) and a **shorter edition** (£25) in one volume. It is also available on special **DVD version**, with one year's free automatic updates from the Internet, for only £35. Get the THE WORLDWIDE ENCYCLOPAEDIA for your home and you'll wonder how your family ever managed without it. AVAILABLE NOW at Ashworth Bookshops Ltd. I guarantee that if you are not completely satisfied within 28 days, I will give you a full refund.

M Russell

M. Russell
Ashworth Bookshops

OVER 500,000 COPIES SOLD

2 Here are Margaret Russell's notes about *The Complete Collection of Business Letters*. Look back at Nigel Westwood's letter in 8.1 and the letter about *The Worldwide Encyclopaedia* above and write her circular sales letter.

The Complete Collection of Business Letters

- special low price
- index of **3,000** ready-to-use letters
- accompanying CD-ROM
- adapt, click and print or
  adapt, click and email

- what took hours, now takes minutes
- hardback £38
- paperback £22
- both include CD-ROM

8.6 An invitation

After she sent her order to Universal Books, Ms Russell received a formal invitation to the launch of *The Worldwide Encyclopaedia*. She checked her diary. Can she attend the launch? Write Ms Russell's reply.

ORGANISER SUPER PC

SEPTEMBER 6 Wednesday

8
9 9–12 Sales conference
10 HQ
11
12
13
14 Brief Jim on next week
15
16 To airport 16.30
17
18 Flight ZR345 18.55
19 Holiday
20

THE DIRECTOR OF
UNIVERSAL BOOKS LTD
HAS THE PLEASURE OF INVITING

Ms M. Russell

TO THE LAUNCH OF
THE WORLDWIDE ENCYCLOPAEDIA
AT THE ROYAL HOTEL
345 THE STRAND
LONDON EC10 6HY
AT 20.00 ON 6 SEPTEMBER, 2006

RSVP
MR P. ENGL UNIVERSAL BOOKS
TEL 01534 797201

8.7 Some bad news

Some days later, Margaret Russell received some bad news from Nigel Westwood. Fill in the missing words or phrases.

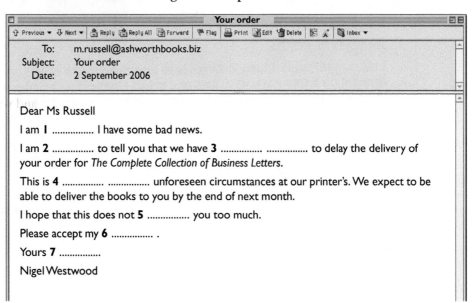

Your order

Previous ▾ Next ▾ | Reply Reply All Forward | Flag | Print Edit Delete | Inbox ▾

To: m.russell@ashworthbooks.biz
Subject: Your order
Date: 2 September 2006

Dear Ms Russell

I am **1** .... I have some bad news.

I am **2** .... to tell you that we have **3** .... to delay the delivery of your order for *The Complete Collection of Business Letters*.

This is **4** .... unforeseen circumstances at our printer's. We expect to be able to deliver the books to you by the end of next month.

I hope that this does not **5** .... you too much.

Please accept my **6** ....

Yours **7** ....

Nigel Westwood

8.8 Complaining

When Margaret Russell received Nigel Westwood's email, she was very angry. She decided to write a strong complaint and send it by fax. Write her fax, using these notes.

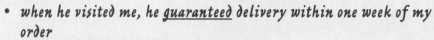

- when he visited me, he _guaranteed_ delivery within one week of my order
- his email of **23 August** confirmed this
- I have already paid **50%** of the total cost!
- demand immediate delivery
- warn him about legal action

8.9 A reply and an apology

The next day, Margaret Russell received this fax. What has happened to her deposit?

13:26 3-09-2006   FROM: UNIVERSAL BOOKS, JERSEY   01534 797407

Your ref
Our ref. NW/lea

FAX MESSAGE

To: M. Russell
Manager, Ashworth Bookshops

Fax: 01272 782422

3 September 2006

Universal Books Ltd

PO Box 379 Jersey,
Channel Islands

Tel. 01534-797201
Fax 01534-797407

books@universal.net
www.universal.net

Thank you for your fax.

I regret to tell you that Nigel Westwood is no longer working for us, and I can find no record of the money you say you have paid to him. I have passed your fax to the Jersey Police who are investigating a number of other cases concerning Mr Westwood.
Mr Westwood himself seems to have disappeared, although the police believe he may be somewhere in France.

I suggest you contact the police yourself and register your claim against Mr Westwood.

I am sorry I cannot help you more.

Yours sincerely

Pablo Engl

Pablo Engl
Director, Universal Books.

8B Activity section   A trade fair

1 Paolo Fellini and Corina Lombardo, from Massari Tractors Ltd, recently visited their agent in India, Sujit Singh of Agricultural Supplies Ltd. They talked about the low sales of Massari Tractors. Mr Singh said he would put his ideas in an email. Read the message he sent Paolo Fellini and answer these questions.

a Why does Mr Singh think that a drop in price of 8% is enough to increase sales?
b Why does he want Massari Tractors to pay for advertising?
c How does Mr Singh ask if Massari can lower their prices? What would he write if he wanted them to do the following?
   i   give a greater discount
   ii increase the length of the guarantee
   iii give a free gift with every tractor

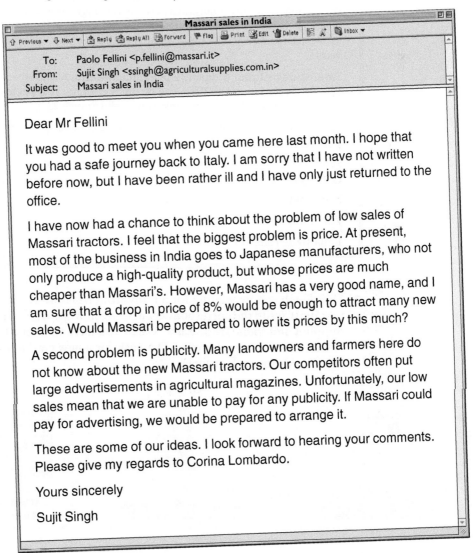

Massari sales in India

To: Paolo Fellini <p.fellini@massari.it>
From: Sujit Singh <ssingh@agriculturalsupplies.com.in>
Subject: Massari sales in India

Dear Mr Fellini

It was good to meet you when you came here last month. I hope that you had a safe journey back to Italy. I am sorry that I have not written before now, but I have been rather ill and I have only just returned to the office.

I have now had a chance to think about the problem of low sales of Massari tractors. I feel that the biggest problem is price. At present, most of the business in India goes to Japanese manufacturers, who not only produce a high-quality product, but whose prices are much cheaper than Massari's. However, Massari has a very good name, and I am sure that a drop in price of 8% would be enough to attract many new sales. Would Massari be prepared to lower its prices by this much?

A second problem is publicity. Many landowners and farmers here do not know about the new Massari tractors. Our competitors often put large advertisements in agricultural magazines. Unfortunately, our low sales mean that we are unable to pay for any publicity. If Massari could pay for advertising, we would be prepared to arrange it.

These are some of our ideas. I look forward to hearing your comments. Please give my regards to Corina Lombardo.

Yours sincerely

Sujit Singh

2 Shortly after he sent the email, both Agricultural Supplies and Massari Tractors received this circular email about a New Delhi fair. Read it and answer these questions.

a Why is it necessary to book early?

b How can the organisers help overseas companies to come?

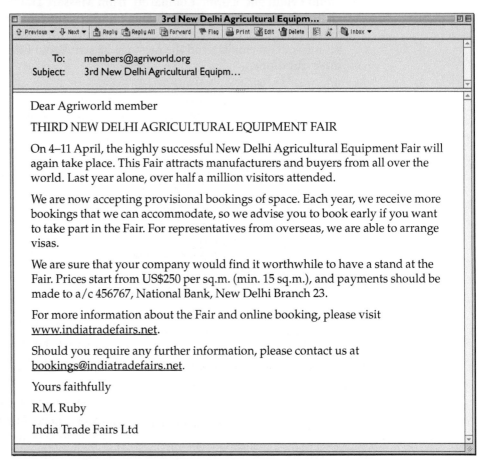

3 Sujit Singh is now waiting for a reply from Massari Tractors. In three groups, you must write the correspondence between Massari Tractors, Agricultural Supplies and India Trade Fairs. When you have written a letter, email or fax, 'send' it to the correct group. Then ask for a new card number. (There are three cards for each group.)

Group 1	Group 2	Group 3

8C The writing process   Checking your work (3)

In Section 6C, you looked at accuracy in your writing, and in Section 7C, you looked at style and levels of formality. Here, you can look at the *way* your message is written: Is it clear? Does it say what you want it to say?

1 A clear message

Even if a letter or email is in correct English, it can still be difficult to understand and follow. What can make a message unclear, do you think?

Brainstorm your ideas with other students, then compare with the points on page 123.

An unclear message

2 Are they clear?

Read these messages. Are they clear? What is the problem with each one? Can you write a better version of each message?

a

Dear Ms Wilson

Thank you for your telephone call.

I have arranged for you to have a meeting with Susan Lander and a separate meeting with Diana Dell on 15 November. You can meet her at 11 a.m. Unfortunately, she cannot go to lunch with you, as they have to attend a sales conference.

With best wishes

b

Dear Ms Brown

I am writing to cancel my order.

Please can you cancel my order because I do not need the things any more.

Yours faithfully

c

Dear Mr Smith

Thank you for your email. Here are directions for getting to our office.

When you arrive at the airport, take a bus to the train station. From the station, walk down the road in front of you and turn left. Walk to the end of the road and there is a supermarket. Turn right there, and our building is in front of you. I will wait for you at the main door. When you arrive at the train station, please telephone us. The airport buses leave from the side of the airport. Turn right when you come out from Passport Control.

Looking forward to meeting you,

Role cards

---

1 Reply to Mr Mizuno. Tell him if you can meet him on 13 March (see your diary on card 27).

Message plan
- put a subject heading
- say what you are writing about
- tell him if you can meet him or not (give the day and time)
- recommend the Hotel Bluebird to him (tell him where it is – see map)
- ask him to let you know where he will be staying in case you need to contact him
- close the message

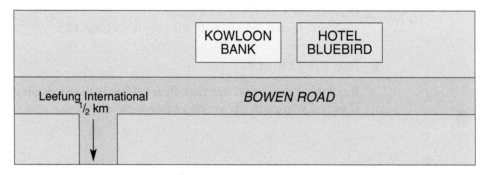

---

2 You are Ms D. Hicks, the Purchasing Supervisor at the Court Hotel. You have just received this memo from your manager.

THE COURT HOTEL

MEMORANDUM

DATE 1 February

FROM Manager

SUBJECT Slembrouck BVBA Order 256

TO Purchasing Supervisor

We have just received this order. Unfortunately, we ordered 1,000 bottles of orange juice, and they have sent us 1,000 bottles of shampoo. We need the juice for a wedding party in two weeks' time.

Please email Slembrouck BVBA and ask them to deliver the juice that we ordered as soon as possible. They can collect the shampoo at the same time. Their email address is info@slembrouck.be.

3 You are the Production Supervisor at Leefung Plastics (Singapore) Ltd. Here is your diary for 10 March and a map showing where your factory is.

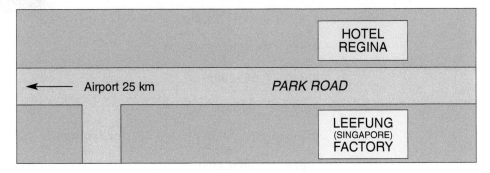

Reply to Nagakura.

Message plan
- put a subject heading
- thank Mr Mizuno for his message (say what it was about)
- say if you can or cannot meet him (give the day and time)
- give him the information that he wanted
- close the message

4 You are Sujit Singh, from Agricultural Supplies Ltd. Reply to the circular email from India Trade Fairs Ltd.

Message plan
- ask them to provisionally reserve 30 square metres
- tell them that your supplier, Massari Tractors, will probably come
- ask them to arrange a visa for Corina Lombardo (give the following information: Full name: Corina Rosanna Lombardo; Nationality: Italian; Passport number: 34768C)

5 You have just checked your stock levels of Alpha Rapid Bottlers. This is the information you found.

```
STOCK CONTROL MANAGER v5.1

Date:  7-06-2006

Part no:  675162

Description:  Alpha Rapid Bottler (complete system)

Stock:  1 available

Next stock:  expected 9-12 months
```

Write to Jarritos and tell them this.

Message plan
- say what you are writing about
- tell them the information you have
- ask them to tell you as soon as possible if they want the bottling system

---

6 Your business is in serious financial difficulties. You owe £250,000, so you cannot settle your account with Lumino Inks. (The bank refused your last cheque.) To stop legal action against you, your lawyers, Smith & Sons, have told you to go into liquidation. They will write to all the companies involved soon.

1 Write to Lumino Inks.

Message plan
- refer to their message
- tell them about your present situation
- give the bad news about their bill
- say what you have had to do
- tell them about your lawyers
- apologise and close the message

2 Write a short message to Northern Paperworks telling them about your present situation and what you have had to do.

7 You work in the Sales Department of Midtec Cables Ltd. You have received a message from Tavridis Ltd, asking for information. Send them a message with the following details:

20,000 metres of 15-amp cable at 24p a metre	£4,800
less 8% for a large order	– £ 384
	£4,416
packing and freight	£ 270
C&F TOTAL	£4,686

You can deliver the cable ten weeks after you have received their letter of credit.

Message plan
• refer to their message
• give the information

---

8 You are Charlotte McEvoy from Western Travel. Mr Thomas has sent you this newspaper article. He wants to know what will happen if Pekar Airways collapses while his group is in Mexico or before they go on holiday. Write to Sun Express and ask them.

Pekar Airways collapse fear

THE DIRECTOR of Pekar Airways said last night that the company is in serious financial difficulties. This follows a meeting with the representatives of Northern Bank. The bank has agreed to give Pekar one more month to make interest payments. This is the third time that the bank has agreed to delay Pekar's repayments.

Pekar's problems began when the airline bought four Concorde planes from British Airways just over a year ago. Pekar expected to find business in organising short flights at above the speed of sound. Unfortunately

Message plan
• refer to the booking
• say that Mr Thomas has given you a newspaper article (say what it is about)
• ask them to tell you exactly what will happen if Pekar collapses
• close the message

---

9 The bank has just telephoned you. They cannot pay the cheque from Wainman Ltd because there is no money in the account. Write to Wainman Ltd and tell them this. Demand payment in cash. Warn them about legal action.

Memorandum

Date: 14 February

From: Manager

Subject: Slembrouck BVBA

To: Purchasing & Sales Supervisor

I am very surprised that Slembrouck BVBA are not going to deliver the coffee and the rest of the tea until the end of the month. We have now found a new supplier, so please cancel our order with them.

You can also tell them that we are sorry, but we do not intend to do any more business with them.

11

Memorandum

To: Sales Dept

Date: 20 October

From: Marketing Dept

Ref: Stock order DG 00315

Subject: cable prices

The price of the 15-amp cable has been reduced.
The price is now 22p a metre, less any normal discounts.

**MIDTEC
CABLES LTD**

Write to Tavridis Ltd and tell them this.

Message plan
- refer to your last message (say what you are writing about)
- give the good news
- ask them to tell you as soon as possible if they now want to order

12 This surveyor's report has just arrived in the post.

REPORT
ON THE EXPLOSION AT PERFECTA LTD
SUMMARY

We have examined the heating system at Perfecta. In our opinion, the wrong oil was put in the heating unit. This caused the central-heating unit to overheat and explode. We found nothing wrong with the heating system itself or the way it was installed.

Write to Bauer AG.

Message plan
- apologise for blaming them
- ask them to fit a new heating system as soon as possible
- close the message and apologise again

Remember to refer to any message you have received from them.

---

13 If you have not had a reply from Massari Tractors, send them a short email asking them to reply (the final date for payment is soon).
If Massari Tractors agree to pay half the cost, write an email to India Trade Fairs Ltd, confirming your booking.

Message plan
- confirm how much space you will need
- tell them you will pay direct to their account (see their circular letter for details)
- tell them when Corina Lombardo will arrive
- you will contact them again then

---

14 Reply to India Trade Fairs Ltd.

Message plan
- thank them for their email
- tell them who is responsible for all advertising and promotion in the New Delhi area (they should contact them)
- Corina Lombardo will go to the fair (ask them to arrange her visa, details as follows: full name: Corina Rosanna Lombardo; passport: Italian, 34768C):
- you also need to know exactly where the fair will be

09:21   1-JUN-2006   SUN EXPRESS   0870 567 8768

Memorandum

Date: 1 June   **From:** Sales Manager   **To:** all branches

Tour 5210—New Carrier

1. We have found a new carrier for Tour 5210. This is DTL Aviation Company.
2. All clients who still want to take this holiday must reconfirm their booking as soon as possible.
3. They must also check in at Gatwick Airport by 0825 on the day of departure.
4. Please write to all agencies and tell them this.

Message plan
- say exactly what you are writing about (refer to your last message)
- give the good news
- tell them about reconfirming
- tell them about the check-in time
- close the message

16 You have just received this email from your Technical Department.

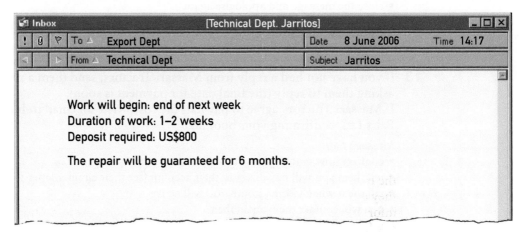

Inbox   [Technical Dept. Jarritos]

| To △ | Export Dept | Date | 8 June 2006 | Time | 14:17 |
| From △ | Technical Dept | Subject | Jarritos |

Work will begin: end of next week
Duration of work: 1–2 weeks
Deposit required: US$800

The repair will be guaranteed for 6 months.

Message plan
- thank Mr Sánchez for his message
- tell him the good news about when the repair will start
- tell him how long the repair will take
- ask him to pay the deposit before you begin the work
- tell him about the guarantee

17 Your factory is closed due to the cold weather. This is costing you over €50,000 a day. It is extremely important that you get a new heating unit as soon as possible. Write to Aqua Warm BV (Beulingstraat 23, Amsterdam, The Netherlands) to find out when they can deliver a new one and at what price. Remember, you need this heating unit urgently.

Message plan
- say what you are writing about
- tell them what has happened
- tell them about your factory now
- ask them for the information you need

18

THE COURT HOTEL

MEMORANDUM

DATE 11 February	*SUBJECT* Slembrouck BVBA Order 256
FROM Manager	*TO* Purchasing Supervisor

We still have not received the orange juice from Slembrouck BVBA.

Please email ABC (Drinks Machines) Ltd, abc@abcdrinks.com, and ask if they can help us. Tell them that we ordered the juice from Slembrouck, but they sent us the wrong goods. We need 1,000 small bottles immediately. Ask them if they have these available, and if so, what their prices are.

19 If you are still waiting for the information about the cable from one or both of the manufacturers, send a fax asking them to reply. Keep sending faxes until they do reply. You need the information urgently. When you have the information that you need (prices and delivery time) from both manufacturers, ask for a new card number.
Contact details are: Hanston Electrics fax +44 161 565342; Midtec Cables Ltd fax +44 1392 929610.

20 The following fax has come from head office.

Memorandum

Date: 30 May   **From:** Sales Manager   **To:** all branches

Collapse of Pekar Airways

1. Pekar Airways, our carrier for tours to Mexico, has collapsed. This means that Tour 5210 is now cancelled.
2. Please write to all agencies and tell them we will refund their deposits as soon as possible.

Message plan
- say exactly what you are writing about
- give the bad news (say what you have had to do)
- tell them about their deposits
- close the message

---

21 You are Tony Smith. You work in the Export Sales Department at Wesco. You have just received this email from your Technical Department.

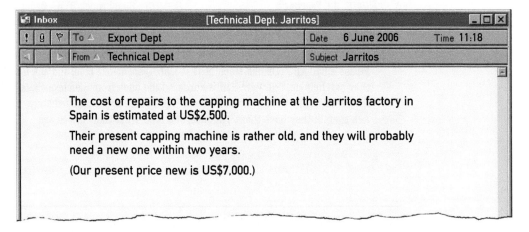

Inbox — [Technical Dept. Jarritos]

To Export Dept   Date 6 June 2006   Time 11:18
From Technical Dept   Subject Jarritos

The cost of repairs to the capping machine at the Jarritos factory in Spain is estimated at US$2,500.

Their present capping machine is rather old, and they will probably need a new one within two years.

(Our present price new is US$7,000.)

Write to Mr Sánchez and tell him this.

Message plan
- mention the dinner you had with him and the visit to his factory
- give the quotation
- say why the price is high
- make the point about the age of the machine
- tell him the price of a new machine
- mention Cristina Barrios

22 This email has just come from your Senior Sales Manager.

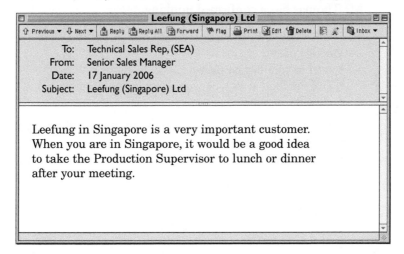

To: Technical Sales Rep, (SEA)
From: Senior Sales Manager
Date: 17 January 2006
Subject: Leefung (Singapore) Ltd

Leefung in Singapore is a very important customer.
When you are in Singapore, it would be a good idea
to take the Production Supervisor to lunch or dinner
after your meeting.

Write to invite the Production Supervisor to lunch.

Message plan
- put a subject heading
- open the message (mention any communication you have received from him/her)
- invite him/her to lunch
- close the message

---

23 You work in the Production Department at Perfecta Ltd, 61 Bath Road, Worcester, WR5 3AB, England. Write a letter to Bauer AG (Altenberg, 5253 Effingen, Switzerland), making a strong complaint about the explosion. Demand compensation.

Message plan
- say what has happened
- make the point that you wrote to them before
- demand that they replace the heating system and pay for your damaged stock (say how much it was valued at)

---

24 If you have *not* received a credit reference from Lumino Inks, send them a short fax asking them to reply (fax no: 01539 467723). When you have received the reference from Lumino Inks, decide if you will let Wainman Ltd buy paper from you on credit.
Note: Look at the names of the directors on Wainman's letter (page 74) and the name of the person at Pelican Paper Ltd (page 75).
Write to Wainman Ltd and tell them what you have decided.

Message plan
- say what you are writing about
- give the good/bad news
- if you give good news: ask them to tell you how much paper they want
- if you give bad news: say you can supply them if they pay in cash

25 It is now two weeks before the holiday should begin. You must make sure that Mr Thomas has a confirmed booking.

1 Write a short message to confirm any booking you have made.

Message plan
- refer to your last message
- give the good news (you would like to book/confirm …)
- close the message

2 Write a short message to the other company, telling them that you have already made a booking.

Message plan
- refer to your last message
- give the bad news
- close the message

---

26 You have just received this memo from the Production Manager.

Memorandum

To: Sales Dept   Ref: Part no. A7B15

Date: 20 October   Subject: Delivery time for 15-amp cable

From: Production Manager

A fire has destroyed part of the factory that supplies us with plastic covering for the 15-amp cable.

This means that there will be a delay of at least six weeks in the delivery of any order for this cable.

Write to Tavridis Ltd and tell them this.

Message plan
- refer to your last message (say what you are writing about)
- give the bad news
- apologise

27 You work in the International Relations Section at Leefung Plastics (International) Ltd in Hong Kong. Here is your diary for 12 and 13 March and the addresses of your other factories.

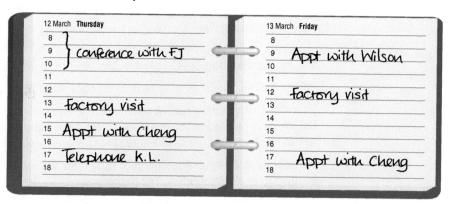

12 March Thursday	13 March Friday
8	8
9 ⎫ conference with FJ	9 Appt with Wilson
10 ⎭	10
11	11
12	12 factory visit
13 factory visit	13
14	14
15 Appt with Cheng	15
16	16
17 Telephone K.L.	17 Appt with Cheng
18	18

> *Leefung factories in SE Asia:*
> Leefung Plastics (Indonesia) Ltd, 77 Jalan Rasuma Said, Jakarta, Indonesia.
> Manager: S. Mardaung
> Leefung Plastics (Singapore) Ltd, Box 226, Brown St PO, Singapore.
> Manager: M. Chew
> Leefung Plastics (Thailand) Ltd, 48 Ramkhamhang Road, Bangkok, Thailand.
> Manager: P. Hemsuchi
> Leefung Plastics (Malaysia) Ltd, PO Box 2454, Kuala Lumpur, Malaysia.
> Manager: M. Razi

Reply to Nagakura's emails.

Message plan
- put a subject heading
- thank Mr Mizuno for his emails (say what they were about)
- say if you can or cannot meet him (give the day and time)
- give him the information he wanted
- close the email

---

28 Write to Massari Tractors about the Agricultural Equipment Fair.

Message plan
- tell them you have reserved some space (say how much)
- you need this much space for a tractor
- say how much it costs
- say why you think it is important to have a stand at the fair
- ask if Massari Tractors can pay half the cost

29   You work in the Project Planning Department at Bauer AG, Altenberg, 5253 Effingen, Switzerland. You have just received this memo from the General Manager.

·MEMORANDUM·MEMORANDUM·MEMORANDUM·MEMORANDUM·

TO: Project Planning Dept   DATE: Jan. 4

FROM: GM   SUBJECT: Aqua Warm BV

I am sure that you have read about the recent explosion at Perfecta Ltd. We have decided not to install any more Aqua Warm central-heating systems until we can be sure that they are absolutely safe.

Please write and inform Aqua Warm of this. Their address is Beulingstraat 23, Amsterdam, The Netherlands.

BAUER AG

Message plan
- say what you are writing about
- give the bad news

---

30   You are the Purchasing and Sales Supervisor at ABC (Drinks Machines) Ltd. You have just received this memo from your manager.

Memorandum

Date: 1 February   Subject: Slembrouck BVBA

From: Manager   To: Purchasing & Sales Supervisor

Slembrouck BVBA recently delivered our order No. 260. Unfortunately, we ordered 150 kilos of tea and coffee powder, and they only sent us 75 kilos of tea.

We need the coffee and the rest of the tea at once. Please email them and ask them to deliver this as soon as possible. Their email address is info@slembrouck.be.

31 You are the Sales Supervisor at Golden Holidays. You recently sent some information to Western Travel. Write a follow-up message to them, telling them that you can now offer a 10% reduction on the price of your holidays to Mexico. (There has been a change in the exchange rate.)

Message plan
- say what you are writing about (refer to your last message)
- give the good news
- give the reason
- close the message

32 This email has just arrived.

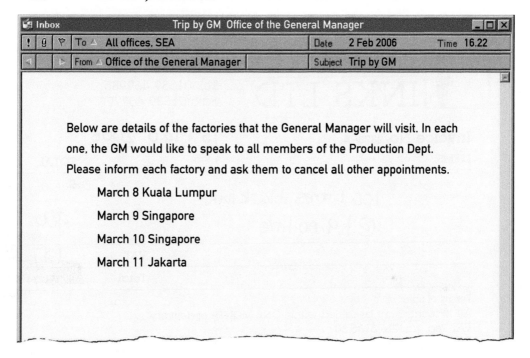

Write to Leefung Plastics in Singapore and tell them this.

Message plan
- put a subject heading
- say what you are writing about (GM's forthcoming trip)
- say when the GM will be in Singapore
- say who he wants to talk to while he is there
- ask them to cancel all appointments
- close the message

33 If you have not heard from Tavridis Ltd, send them a short fax asking them if they now want to place an order.
When they have told you that they want to order, write to confirm their order. Give them the payment details.

Message plan
- refer to their message or fax (thank them)
- ask them to open a letter of credit in your favour for £4,318
- ask them to arrange for a bank in England to guarantee the l/c

---

34 You are Claire Brown at Lumino Inks. You sent this invoice to Wainman Ltd six months ago, and they have not paid.

LUMINO INKS LTD

Main Street
Kendal LA9 6TW

Tel: 01539 469985
Fax: 01539 467723

Invoice No 2323-A   **15 May 2006**

ITEMS		TOTAL £	
100 Litres, black ink @ £9.00 litre		900	—
	VAT	157	50
	Total	1057	50

Terms of sale:
All accounts must be settled within ONE MONTH of delivery
VAT Reg. No. 216 3185 80

This is the third time they have broken your terms of sale. Write and ask for payment now.

Message plan
- say what you are writing about
- ask for payment
- make the point about the terms of sale

35 Send an email to Agricultural Supplies Ltd, saying that you will pay half the cost of a stand at the fair and that Corina Lombardo will arrive on 2 April. She will stay at the Hilton Hotel and will contact them when she arrives.

36

Memo

Date: 14 February

From: Manager

Subject: Order No. 260

To: Sales Supervisor

Please write and tell ABC (Drinks Machines) Ltd that we are sorry that we did not send any coffee to them. Our delivery vans will be in their area at the end of this month. We can deliver the coffee and the rest of the tea then.

We can give them a special discount price of €4.50 per kilo for the coffee because of the problems we have caused.

37 You are Raul Sánchez, General Manager, Jarritos SA.
Send faxes or emails to both Alpha (+33-56 81 38 58 29, sales@alpha.fr) and Wesco (+44 117 973 4261, support@wesco.co.uk).

Message plan
Ask them:
• when they can begin the repairs / install the new system
• how long the work will take
• to reply as soon as possible

Keep sending faxes or emails until they reply. When you have received messages from both companies, ask for a new card number.

Memorandum

To: Sales Dept   Ref: Part no. A7B15

Date: 22 October   Subject: Delivery time for 15-amp cable

From: Production Manager

We have been able to find a new supplier for the plastic covering for the 15-amp cable.

Delivery time is now back to normal. However, there is a small increase in price. The cable is now 23p a metre, less the normal discounts.

Write to Tavridis Ltd and tell them this. Ask them if they can tell you as soon as possible if they want to order.

Message plan
- refer to your last message
- give the good news
- give the bad news
- ask them to tell you if they want to order

---

39 Write to your friend, Robert White, at Northern Paperworks. He wants a credit reference on Wainman Ltd. Tell him about your experience with them. You have also heard that they are in serious financial difficulties. Tell Robert White if you think he should give Wainman Ltd credit or not.

---

40 You have just seen this article in the newspaper. Decide what you are going to do and then:
- send faxes or emails to make sure you have a working bottling system
- send any necessary emails or letters to cancel an order you have made.

Message plan
- say what you are writing about
- give the bad news
- give the reason
- say what you are going to do instead

New law against disposable bottles

THE government has passed a new law forbidding the use of disposable bottles for soft drinks from the end of next year. The new law aims to reduce the amount of pollution caused by bottles thrown away

41 The following email has arrived.

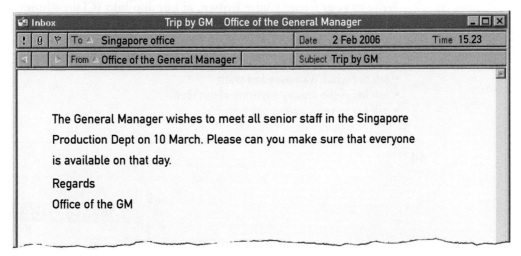

Write to Nagakura and cancel your meeting with Jun Mizuno.

Message plan
- put a subject heading
- say you are sorry to tell him that you have to cancel the appointment (give the day and time)
- say why
- close the message

---

42 If you have *not* received a booking, write and tell Western Travel that you only have a few places left.

Message plan
- put a heading
- say exactly what you are writing about
- tell them about the places
- tell them that, if they want to book, they must do it as soon as possible
- close the message

If you *have* received a booking, write to Western Travel and give them the instructions for joining the holiday.

Message plan
- say exactly what you are writing about
- ask them to tell all clients to check in at Gatwick Airport by 0830 on the day of departure
- close the message

43 You are Robert White at Northern Paperworks.
Write to your friend Claire Brown, at Lumino Inks (Claire@luminoinks.co.uk),
to ask her for a credit reference on Wainman Ltd.

Message plan
- introduce your message (*I was wondering …*)
- tell her what Wainman Ltd want
- ask her if she knows anything about them
- ask her to reply as soon as possible

44

Memo

Date: 11 February   *Subject:* Order No. 256

From: Manager   *To:* Sales Supervisor

Please write and tell the Court Hotel that we are sorry
that we made a mistake with their order. (Instead of 1,000
bottles of orange juice, we sent 1,000 bottles of shampoo!)
Their email address is manager@courthotel.co.uk.

Our delivery vans will be in their area at the beginning of
next month. We will deliver the juice then and collect the
shampoo.

45 If you have not heard from the company that you want to order from, send a
short fax asking them for a reply.
You should receive some new information from both companies. Send any
necessary letters, emails or faxes to cancel, confirm or place your order. You
must be sure that you will get the cable that you need.

46 You work in the Consumer Relations Department at Aqua Warm BV, Beulingstraat 23, Amsterdam, The Netherlands. You have just received this email message from the General Manager.

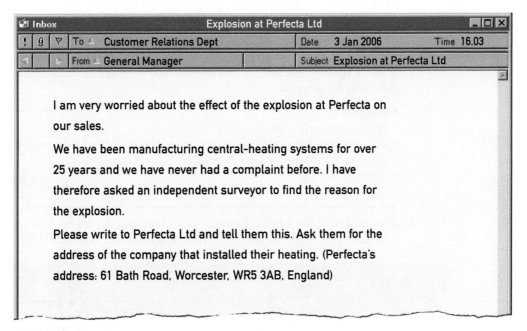

Inbox	Explosion at Perfecta Ltd	_ □ ✕
! 0 ▽ To △ Customer Relations Dept	Date 3 Jan 2006	Time 16.03
◁ ▷ From △ General Manager	Subject Explosion at Perfecta Ltd	

I am very worried about the effect of the explosion at Perfecta on our sales.

We have been manufacturing central-heating systems for over 25 years and we have never had a complaint before. I have therefore asked an independent surveyor to find the reason for the explosion.

Please write to Perfecta Ltd and tell them this. Ask them for the address of the company that installed their heating. (Perfecta's address: 61 Bath Road, Worcester, WR5 3AB, England)

Message plan
- say what you are writing about
- make the point about Aqua Warm's past history
- tell them about the surveyor
- ask them for the address of the company that installed the heating

---

47 You are Paolo Fellini. Reply to Sujit Singh.

Message plan
- thank him for his email and say something about his illness
- you cannot reduce your prices any more, as you already give 26% discount
- your sales agreement with Agricultural Supplies Ltd says they will pay for all advertising in the New Delhi area
- however, you can pay part of the cost of a stand at the forthcoming Agricultural Equipment Fair if they think it is a good idea

48 If you have heard from Golden Holidays, write and tell them that you have booked with Sun Express.

Message plan
- refer to their message
- give the bad news
- close the message

If Sun Express have *not* replied to your last message, write to them again and ask them for a reply.

Message plan
- refer to your last message
- say your customer, Mr Thomas, is worried about what will happen if Pekar collapses
- ask them for a reply as soon as possible
- close the message

---

49 You are Françoise Molet, Export Sales Department, Alpha Food Machines. You have just received this email message from the Technical Department.

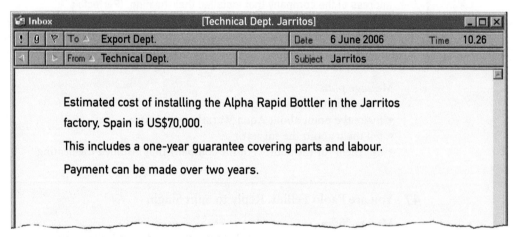

Inbox	[Technical Dept. Jarritos]				
!	To △ Export Dept.	Date	6 June 2006	Time	10.26
	From △ Technical Dept.	Subject	Jarritos		

Estimated cost of installing the Alpha Rapid Bottler in the Jarritos factory, Spain is US$70,000.

This includes a one-year guarantee covering parts and labour.

Payment can be made over two years.

Write to Mr Sánchez and tell him this.

Message plan
- mention the dinner you had with him and the visit to his factory
- give the quotation
- tell him about the guarantee and payment
- mention Cristina Barrios

50 You should now have received a quotation from both companies. You have US$5,000 for maintenance expenses. Your profits each year are US$60,000. Decide if you want to:

a repair the capping machine
b buy a new capping machine
c buy an Alpha Rapid Bottler.

Then write a fax or email to the right company, accepting their quotation.

Message plan
- refer to their last message
- say you are pleased to accept their quotation for …
- ask them to start work as soon as possible
- ask them when that will be

51

Memorandum

Date: 11 February   Subject: Court Hotel

From: Manager   To: Purchasing & Sales Supervisor

I have recently heard from Mr Wilson at Western Trading Co. that the Court Hotel need a large quantity of orange juice at once.

We have a large supply of juice that we do not need. Our price is €45 per 100 bottles. Please email the Court Hotel and tell them that we would be happy to supply them if they can tell us how many bottles they need. Their email address is manager@courthotel.co.uk.

52 If you have *not* received a booking from Agricultural Supplies Ltd, send a follow-up email, similar to the email that you sent Massari Tractors. If you *have* received a booking from Agricultural Supplies Ltd, write an email confirming their booking.

Message plan
- confirm how much space you have reserved
- tell them they must pay by 3 March
- payments to a/c 456767, National Bank, Mahatma Gandhi Road Branch, New Delhi

LUMINO INKS LTD

Main Street
Kendal LA9 6TW
Tel: 01539 469985
Fax: 01539 467723

Invoice No 2323–A   15 May 2006

ITEMS	TOTAL £	
100 Litres, black ink @ £9.00 litre	900	—
VAT	157	50
Total	1057	50

Terms of sale:
All accounts must be settled within ONE MONTH of delivery
VAT Reg. No. 216 3185 80

You received this invoice six months ago, but you could not pay then because you were waiting for payment from your customers. However, you can now pay. Write to Ms Claire Brown at Lumino Inks (you do not know her).

Message plan
- say what you are writing about
- tell her that you are sending a cheque separately by post
- apologise for the delay
- give the reason

54 You are the Booking Supervisor at Sun Express. You have received a booking from Western Travel for 25 people. Write a message confirming the booking and giving further information.

Message plan
- say that you have booked a holiday for 25 people (give the tour number and departure date)
- ask Western Travel to tell their clients that they must check in at Gatwick Airport at 0930
- close the message

55 Write to Massari Tractors and confirm that you have reserved some space for their agent. Also tell them that you have arranged a visa for Corina Lombardo. She can collect it at the airport. Tell them where the fair will be.

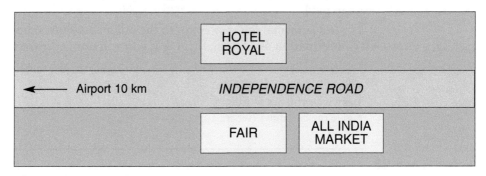

56

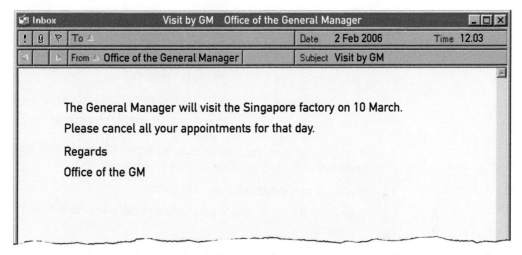

Write to Nagakura. Tell Mr Mizuno that you cannot meet him on 10 March. Your assistant, Helen Cheng, can meet him.

Message plan
- put a subject heading
- say what you are writing about (his forthcoming visit)
- say, unfortunately, you will not be available when he comes (say why)
- tell him about Ms Cheng
- ask him to confirm if he would like to meet her
- close the message

If you have received a message from Mr Mizuno, remember to include an answer in your message to him.

57 You should now have all the information from both companies. Decide which company you are going to buy from and then quickly:

1 send a short *fax* to one company ordering the cable (ask for details of how to pay)

2 send a normal *letter or email* to the other company, thanking them for the information and telling them that you will not order from them.

Message plan
- put a heading
- say why you are writing
- give the bad news (where appropriate)

58

THE COURT HOTEL
MEMORANDUM

DATE 14 February   *SUBJECT* ABC (Drinks Machines) Ltd

FROM Manager   *TO* Purchasing Supervisor

If you have not heard from ABC (Drinks Machines) Ltd, please email them again and ask them if they have received your message.

If ABC Ltd have the juice that we need, please:

1. email them and ask them to send us 1,000 small bottles as soon as possible;

2. email Slembrouck BVBA and cancel our order with them. Tell them that we have found a new supplier for the orange juice and ask them to collect their shampoo as soon as possible. You can also tell them that we do not intend to do any further business with them.

59

MEMORANDUM

TO: Consumer Relations   DATE: 6 Jan.

FROM: GM   SUBJECT: Perfecta Ltd

Please find attached a copy of the surveyor's report on the explosion at Perfecta.

This shows that the wrong type of heating oil was used. Please write to Perfecta Ltd and tell them that we cannot give them any compensation. We can however supply a new heating unit immediately at a special 12½% discount price of €26,000.

REPORT

ON THE EXPLOSION AT PERFECTA LTD

SUMMARY

We have examined the heating system at Perfecta. In our opinion, the wrong oil was put in the heating unit. This caused the central-heating unit to overheat and explode. We found nothing wrong with the heating system itself or the way it was installed.

---

60 You work at India Trade Fairs Ltd. Write a follow-up email to Massari Tractors, reminding them about the fair. Look at the circular for some ideas.

Message plan
- say what you are writing about
- give some details of the fair
- tell them there is still some space available (over 150 companies have already booked)
- tell them the prices

---

61 You are Stefaan Ghislain, the Sales Supervisor at Slembrouck BVBA. You have just received this memo from your manager.

Memo

Date: 1 February

From: Manager

Subject: Order No. 260

To: Sales Supervisor

We recently sent part of an order to ABC (Drinks Machines) Ltd. Please write and tell them that we could only send half of the tea that they ordered; we will send the rest of the order by the end of the month. Their email address is abc@abcdrinks.com.

62 You are Jun Mizuno. You have just found this note on your desk.

Telephone Message

date: 15/1   time: 10.30   call taken by: APS

Your travel agent rang. All flights to Hong Kong on 12 March are full. The first available flight arrives at 8.00 a.m. on 13 March. She has booked you on that flight. She also wants to know which hotel you want to stay at.

Write to change your appointment with the International Relations Section at Leefung Plastics (International) Ltd in Hong Kong. Ask them to recommend a hotel to you.

Message plan
• put a subject heading
• say what you are writing about (your forthcoming visit to their company)
• say, unfortunately, you will not be in Hong Kong until 13 March (say why)
• ask if you can meet them on 13 March (at the same time as before)
• ask them about the hotel
• close the message

63 You have received a fax from Tavridis Ltd, asking for information. Send them a fax with the following details:

20,000 metres of 15-amp cable at 22p a metre	£4,400	
less 10% for a large order	–£ 440	
	£3,960	
packing and freight	£ 302	
C&F TOTAL	£4,262	

You can deliver the cable eight weeks after you have received their letter of credit. Your address is Hanston Electrics, 48 Golden Road, Manchester, M11 4NS, sales@hanstonelectrics.com.

Message plan
• refer to their fax
• give the information

64 You are Harold Wainman.
You are very low on stocks of paper. Write to your friend, Paula Robinson, at Northern Paperworks and ask her to tell you as soon as possible if she can help you. (Refer to your last letter.)

65 You have just checked your stock levels of Alpha Rapid Bottlers again. This is the information you found.

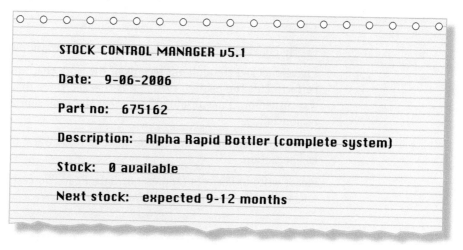

STOCK CONTROL MANAGER v5.1

Date: 9-06-2006

Part no: 675162

Description: Alpha Rapid Bottler (complete system)

Stock: 0 available

Next stock: expected 9-12 months

Write to Jarritos and tell them this.

Message plan
- say what you are writing about
- introduce the bad news
- give the bad news
- tell them that you have put their name on the waiting list
- remind them about the waiting time

66

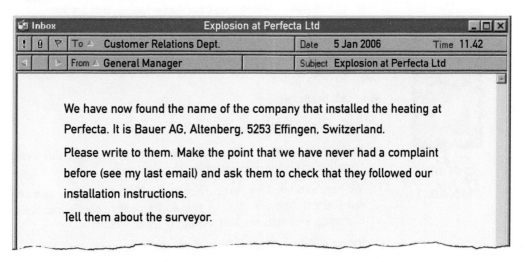

Inbox	Explosion at Perfecta Ltd		
To △ Customer Relations Dept.	Date 5 Jan 2006		Time 11.42
From △ General Manager	Subject Explosion at Perfecta Ltd		

We have now found the name of the company that installed the heating at Perfecta. It is Bauer AG, Altenberg, 5253 Effingen, Switzerland.

Please write to them. Make the point that we have never had a complaint before (see my last email) and ask them to check that they followed our installation instructions.

Tell them about the surveyor.

Remember to refer to any message that you have received from them.

67

TO: GM   DATE: Jan. 5

FROM: Project Planning Dept   SUBJECT: Aqua Warm BV

I have checked through our records of the work that we did at Perfecta Ltd. The heating system was checked three times before it was turned on. I am absolutely sure that the explosion is not our responsibility.

I suggest, therefore, that Perfecta write to Aqua Warm to claim compensation.

Please write to Perfecta (address: 61 Bath Road, Worcester WR5 3AB, England) and explain our position.

BAUER AG

Message plan
- say what you are writing about
- make the point that the system was checked
- suggest that they contact Aqua Warm

Remember to refer to any letter you have received from them.

---

68   **The Sales Manager has just sent you this memo by fax.**

9:36   30-5-2006   FROM: Head Office. Golden Holidays 0870 367 9087

MEMORANDUM

From: Sales Manager

Date: 30-5-2006

To: All branches

Collapse of Pekar Airways

1   Pekar Airways have collapsed. A lot of companies use this airline. We can therefore expect more customers for our tours.

2   We have arranged for our carrier to take 200 extra passengers each week on our tours to Mexico. We can give an immediate confirmed booking to any customer who had booked a holiday using Pekar.

3   Please write to all agencies and tell them this.

Golden Holidays

Message plan
- say exactly what you are writing about
- give the good news
- tell them about the immediate confirmed booking
- close the message

69 Write and tell Wainman Ltd why there is a delay in answering their fax.

Message plan
Explain that:
- Paula Robinson left your company one month ago
- before you allow credit, you normally ask for two references
- you have written to another company and will contact them again soon

70

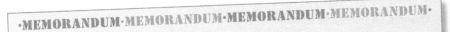

·MEMORANDUM·MEMORANDUM·MEMORANDUM·MEMORANDUM·

TO: GM

DATE: Jan. 6

FROM: Project Planning Dept

SUBJECT: Aqua Warm BV

We have just received the attached surveyor's report.

This shows that Aqua Warm was not responsible for the explosion. We can, therefore, continue to install their heating systems.

Please write and give them this good news.

BAUER AG

REPORT

ON THE EXPLOSION AT PERFECTA LTD

SUMMARY

We have examined the heating system at Perfecta. In our opinion, the wrong oil was put in the heating unit. This caused the central-heating unit to overheat and explode. We found nothing wrong with the heating system itself or the way it was installed.

71 Write and tell Jarritos about this new service.

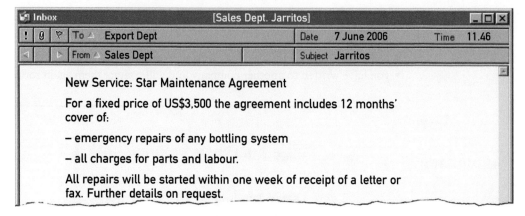

Message plan
- say what you are writing about (their bottling system)
- tell them about the new service

---

72 You have received another telephone message.

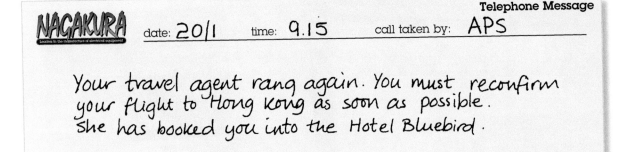

If Leefung Plastics International in Hong Kong have *not* yet told you if they can meet you on 13 March, write and ask them for a reply.

Message plan
- put a subject heading
- say what you are writing about (your message of …)
- ask them if the new day is convenient
- say why you need to know soon (your flight booking)
- close the message

If Leefung International have told you that they can meet you, write a short message to them, telling them where you will be staying if they need to contact you.

Message plan
- mention their last message
- tell them about the hotel
- close the message

Summary of useful phrases and main points

Important! Please see the appropriate unit for details of how each phrase or point is used.

Unit 1 • **Email basics:** see letter and email guide, page 128

• *Dear ... / Yours ...*
Dear Sir or Madam – Yours faithfully
Dear Mr/Mrs/Miss/Ms Smith – Yours sincerely
Dear John – Best wishes

• **Subject heading:** see letter and email guide, page 128

• **Asking for and sending information**
Please can you tell me ...
Please can you send me (details of) ...

• **Thanking for a previous message**
Thank you for your email.
Thank you for your email, dated 6 June.
Many thanks for your message, dated 6 June.
Thank you for your enquiry.

• **Attaching a document**
I am attaching details of ...
I have pleasure in attaching ...
I attach some information which I hope you find useful.
I attach our price list and look forward to hearing from you.

• **Style**
Write in natural style. Do not use an old-fashioned, very formal style.
Do not use very informal language.
Do not use text message abbreviations.
Do not use slang.
Do not use 'emoticons'.
Be polite.

Unit 2 • **Attachments**
I am attaching (our catalogue) to this message.
Please find attached (our report).
I have just received (the photographs), which I have attached to this message.
If you have any problems opening the file, please let me know.

• **Problems with attachments**
I am afraid you forgot to attach the report. Could you send your message again, please?
Unfortunately, the attachment won't open on my computer. Could you send it again in a different format?
Sorry! I forgot to send the attachment.

- **Parts of a message:** see letter and email guide, page 128

- **Beginning a message**
  We are writing to enquire about …
  We are writing in connection with …
  We are interested in … and we would like to know …

  Thank you for your email/letter/fax/call of (date)   {
  We have received your email/letter/fax/call of (date)

  $\left\{\begin{array}{l}\textit{asking if …}\\\textit{enquiring about …}\\\textit{enclosing …}\\\textit{concerning …}\end{array}\right.$

- **Ending a message**
  I look forward to receiving your reply/order/products/etc.
  Looking forward to hearing from you.
  I hope that this information will help you.
  Please contact me if you need further information.
  Please feel free to contact me if you have any further information.
  Please let me know if you need any further information.

- **Email conventions**
  Always open (*Dear …*) and close your emails properly (*Yours …*).
  Don't write in CAPITALS.
  If you are writing a reply to an email, don't copy the original message back.
  Divide your message into paragraphs.
  Check your work before you send it.

Unit 3

- **Referring**
  With reference to …
  Further to …
  I am writing in connection with …
  With regard to …

- **Giving good/bad news**
  good news

I am	*pleased* *delighted* *happy*	*to*	*tell* *inform* *advise*	*you that …*

  bad news

We/I	*regret* *are/am sorry*	*to*	*tell* *inform* *advise*	*you that …*

  We regret that …

- **Saying what you can and cannot do**
  We are unable to …
  We are able to …
  We have been forced to …

- **Giving reasons**

This is	*owing to* *due to* *as a result of* *because of*

- **British English (BE) and American English (AE)**
  AE writers often use a more informal style than BE.
  There are many spelling differences (e.g. *centre/center, colour/color, catalogue/catalog*).
  There are many vocabulary differences (e.g. *curriculum vitae/résumé, post code/zip code, shop/store*).
  There are some grammatical differences (e.g. AE usually uses the past simple where BE uses the present perfect).

- **Paragraphs**
  Most messages are divided into paragraphs. A paragraph can have just one or more sentences in it and it should have one central topic.

Unit 4

- **Letter layout:** see letter and email guide, page 128

- **The date**
  Write the date in full to avoid confusion: *12 June 2006*

- **Making a mild complaint**
  Unfortunately, [then say what is wrong and then request some action].
  Unfortunately, we have not yet received the filing cabinets.

Please could you	
We would be grateful if you could	*deliver them soon.*
We would appreciate it if you could	

- **Making a point**
  I should like to draw your attention to (the fact that) ...
  I should like to point out that ...
  I should like to remind you that ...
  I hope that it is not necessary to remind you that ...

- **Warning**

Unless ... ,	*we will be forced to ...*
If ... (not) ... ,	

- **Making a strong complaint**
  Say exactly what is wrong, make a point connected with this, then demand immediate action:
  It is now over nine months since we placed this order, and we are still waiting for the cabinets. I should like to point out that we have already paid for these cabinets. We must insist, therefore, that you deliver them immediately.
  If you think that it is necessary, you can also give a warning:
  Unless we hear from you within seven days, we will take legal action.

Unit 5

- **Letter layout:** see letter and email guide, page 128

- **Requesting action**

  If it is urgent, add:

Please could you ...	*send us ...*	
We would be grateful if you could ...	*arrange ...*	*as soon as possible.*
	give us further details about ...	*without delay.*
We would appreciate it if you could ...	*let us know (about/if) ...*	*immediately.*
	inform us (about/if) ...	

- **Apologising**
  We must apologise for …
  We apologise for …
  We are extremely sorry for …

- **Fax cover sheets:** see page 52

Unit 6
- **Making a letter or email more personal**
  The three usual parts of a less formal letter or email are:
  – **an opening,** which mentions your feelings about the last contact you had with each other
  – the **main message,** which says why you are writing now and gives the details
  – the **close,** which talks about the future and often mentions some personal information.

- **Personal business letters and emails: the opening**
  Thank you for your letter/telephone call/email/fax.
  It was a pleasure to (see you again at/on …).
  It was good to (hear from you again).
  It was a pity that (we did not have more time to talk at/on …).
  I am sorry that (I missed you when you visited my office).

  After each phrase, you can add a comment:
  Thank you for your letter. It was very interesting to hear about the new developments at Wentol.
  It was good to talk to you on the telephone today. I was sorry to hear that you had not been well.

- **Personal business letters and emails: introducing the topic**

Requesting action	*I was wondering if you could help me.*
Giving information	*I thought you might be interested to hear about …*
Complaining	*I am afraid we have a small problem.*
Giving bad news	*I am afraid I have some bad news.*

- **Personal business letters and emails: the close**
  I look forward to seeing you again next time I am in Taipei.
  If you are ever in London, please give me a ring or stop by my office.
  Please give my regards to Diana Smith.
  Please pass on my best wishes to Mr Lund. I hope that he has now recovered from the flu.

- **Inviting, accepting and declining**

Inviting	*We would be very pleased if you could join us at …*
	We would be delighted if you could come to …
	We have pleasure in inviting you to …
Accepting	*I would be delighted to join you at …*
	I would be very pleased to …
	I am very happy to accept your invitation to …
Declining	*I would very much like to come, but unfortunately …*
	Unfortunately, I will not be able to join you because …
	I am so sorry, but I cannot come to … because …

Unit 7 • **Informal business letters and emails**
In a letter, the name and address of the addressee is sometimes omitted.
Open with the addressee's first name.
Use contractions.
Use short, direct phrases.
Use a friendly style and make personal comments.
Use the language you might use when you are speaking English.
Sign with your first name (not your title).
Use words which are more common, e.g. *ask* (instead of *enquire*), *need* (instead of *require*), *tell* (instead of *advise*).

• **Replying to complaints**
To **accept** a complaint, you can apologise for the problem, explain what caused it, say what action you will take and apologise again.
To **reject** a complaint, you can say you are sorry they had problems, explain why you think it is not your fault, say what you can do (optional) and offer a solution (optional).

• **Advising customers**
To give customers advice, you can say you are sorry you cannot help them directly, say why and suggest what they can do instead:

I recommend that you ...	*contact ...*
You could ...	*try ...*
You might prefer to ...	*use ...*
I suggest you ...	*email ...*

Unit 8 • **Arranging a meeting**
On (date), I will be in your area and I would be grateful if I could meet you.
Would (date) at (time) be convenient for you.
I will telephone you next week to confirm. I look forward to meeting you.

• **Confirming the details of a meeting**
I thought it would be useful to confirm in writing the details of our discussion
and then list the points you discussed:
1 We are able to ...
2 We will ...
3 You will ...

• **Circular letters to promote a product**
Use an appropriate style to attract attention and to create an appropriate image for your product and business.
Use bold or underlining to pick out the **important details**. You can use CAPITAL LETTERS to pick out the name of a product or business.
Divide your message into clearly organised paragraphs. Each paragraph needs to have a clear focus.
Use positive language. Say clearly what your product can do or what it offers.
Show how your product can help the reader or solve a problem for the reader.

Example plans

Unit 2A
Exercise 2.9

Dear Mr Polloni
- Put a subject heading (e.g. *Sodiac cars*).
- Thank him for his telephone call. Say sorry that he had problems with the files.
- Say that you are attaching them again. Tell him to contact you if he still has problems with them.
- Tell him that both cars will be available six months from now. At the moment, you have a special interest-free offer for the first year, and only 5% after that.
- Say you hope that information helps him. Tell him to contact you if he needs further information.
- Close the email.

Yours ...
Name and title

Unit 3A
Exercise 3.9

Dear Sir or Madam
- Put a subject heading.
- Say what you are writing about.
- Give the good/bad news. Give the reason.
- Close the email.

Yours ...
Name and title

Unit 4A
Exercise 4.6

Dear Mr/Ms Onaka
- Put a subject heading.
- Say what you are writing about. Explain that it is not the photocopier that you ordered.
- Ask them to collect it and deliver the correct one.
- Close the letter.

Unit 4A
Exercise 4.11

Dear Sir or Madam
- Put a heading.
- Say what you are writing about (noise).
- Explain exactly what is wrong.
- Make a point connected with this (the contract).
- Demand immediate action.
- Give them a warning.
- Close the letter.

Unit 5A
Exercise 5.6

Dear Mr Langé
- Put a subject heading.
- Say what you are writing about.
- Explain the problem. Apologise.
- Ask him to send his application, CV and photo again by fax.
- Close the letter.

Unit 6A
Exercise 6.9

Dear Ms van Ek
- Put a heading.
- Say it was a pleasure to hear her speak at the course and that her ideas were very interesting.
- Apologise for not being able to come to the workshop. Say you are disappointed.
- Say you would be delighted if she could come to speak at your conference. Give the details.
- Say you look forward to hearing from her.
- Close the email.

Unit 7A
Exercise 7.8

Dear Silvio
- Say how nice it was to meet him last week. Make a comment about it.
- Say you're sorry he has had problems with the ovens. Tell him what you have found out.
- Suggest a solution. Tell him about a newer oven and the discount.
- Say you hope that helps.
- Close the message.

Unit 6C

Some things that you can check:

Punctuation: capital letters, full stops, commas, apostrophes
Spelling: double consonants (e.g. *stopping*), *i* before *e* except after *c* (e.g. *quiet/receive*), *-y* to *-ies* in plurals, silent letters (e.g. *climb*)
Grammar: subject/verb agreement (e.g. *she works*), articles (*the/a*), word order, prepositions, tense, missing words (e.g. verb *be* in *I leaving*)

Unit 8C

Some things that can make a message unclear:

- paragraphs that are too long
- sentences that are too long
- words that are not used very often
- too much information at once
- incomplete information
- information that is in the wrong order

Index of model letters, emails and key words

Letter and email layout guide

1 **A subject heading** helps to focus the reader's attention.

2 **Cc:** send a copy to someone. **Bcc:** send a 'blind copy' (other people can't see that this person has also received a copy). **Attached:** send a file with the message.

3 **The writer's and addressee's references**

4 **The addressee's name and address** is on the left. There is no punctuation at the end of the lines.

5 **The date** is usually on the right.

6 *Dear Sir or Madam* to a company or when you do not know the addressee's name.

7 **Paragraphs** start at the margin. Line space or half line space between each paragraph.

Letters and emails often have three parts:

8 **An opening,** which says why you are writing.

9 **The main message,** which gives the details.

10 **The close,** which usually talks about the future.

11 *Dear Sir or Madam* ends *Yours faithfully. Dear (name)* ends *Yours sincerely* or *Best wishes* (AE *Best regards*).

12 **The writer's name, title and/or department** are at the end.

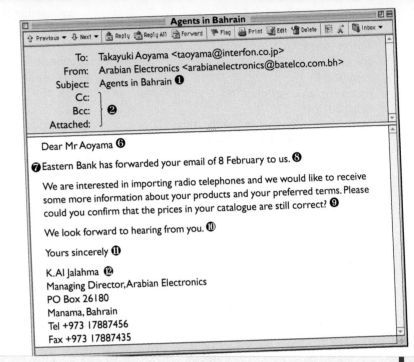

Agents in Bahrain

To: Takayuki Aoyama <taoyama@interfon.co.jp>
From: Arabian Electronics <arabianelectronics@batelco.com.bh>
Subject: Agents in Bahrain ❶
Cc:
Bcc: ❷
Attached:

Dear Mr Aoyama ❻

❼Eastern Bank has forwarded your email of 8 February to us. ❽

We are interested in importing radio telephones and we would like to receive some more information about your products and your preferred terms. Please could you confirm that the prices in your catalogue are still correct? ❾

We look forward to hearing from you. ❿

Yours sincerely ⓫

K. Al Jalahma ⓬
Managing Director, Arabian Electronics
PO Box 26180
Manama, Bahrain
Tel +973 17887456
Fax +973 17887435

Intercity Bank plc

Intercity Bank plc
Jalan Thamin 58
Jakarta 11196
Indonesia
Tel 021 6376008
Fax 021 6376733
www.intercitybank.com/indonesia

Your ref:
Our ref: JL/fh/246 ❸

Mr S. Basuki ❹
Jakarta Furnishings
Jalan Arjuna 7
Jakarta 11190

❺ 30 May 2006

Dear Mr Basuki ❻

Order 2789 ❶

❼ I am writing in connection with your letter of 24 February concerning the above order for some office furniture. ❽

Unfortunately, we have not yet received the filing cabinets which were a part of this order. We would be grateful if you could deliver these as soon as possible or refund our money. ❾

We look forward to hearing from you. ❿

Yours sincerely ⓫

Jennifer Long

Ms Jennifer Long ⓬
Manager